*Jesus and Passover*

Anthony J. Saldarini

# *Jesus and Passover*

*paulist press* ♦*new york*♦*ramsey*

# Contents

*Dedicated*

---

**to my family
with whom I celebrate
the Christian Passover**

# 1

# *Introduction to Passover*

Passover is the Jewish feast most familiar to Christians and most beloved by Jews. The evening Passover meal in every Jewish home with its *matzah* (unleavened bread), candles, symbolic foods, ritual cups of wine, special songs and traditional story of the Exodus from Egypt exudes a mystique which imprints itself on every Jew and fascinates Christians. Families gather, friends are welcomed and the whole Jewish world ceases its ordinary affairs to remember and to hope.

Christians hear about Passover when the story of Israel's redemption from Egypt is read from the Bible or when God is praised for saving Israel. The Easter services refer to Passover often because the Jewish Passover and the Christian celebration of Jesus' death and resurrection grow from the same faith, the same ritual and the same theological tradition. Jesus has saved us as God saved Israel. Many of the symbols are common and the perception of God's loving activity follows a pattern.

Some Christians know the meaning of the word Passover or something of its biblical history. Few appreciate Passover's symbolic power and rich development. Generations of believers have expressed and deepened their faith by living the Passover rituals and reflecting on the Passover story. At Passover the Jewish and later Christian communities hear God and respond, see God and stop in amazement. But what do Christians and Jews share and how can the Christian Easter and Jewish Passover be the same feast?

Like any religious festival Passover expresses who we are and who we want to be. It is a break in the daily routine to live, explore, understand, and enjoy life as it really is, life given to us by another and mysteriously nur-

1

tured in ways we cannot control. Festivals celebrate concrete events or finite manifestations of our God who reveals himself over time, in the places where we live.

Festivals undergo development because the community's perceptions of God and responses to God change. A community's history, experience, self-awareness and continuity lies embedded in its festivals. The past is put to immediate and vital service of the present. Private aspirations and community goals merge in the symbols and metaphors spoken and ritually enacted by the participants.

What a tradition says and the form in which it says it depends on the community which cherishes and nourishes the tradition. The community itself has grown from the tradition and depends on it for sustenance; at the same time it personifies the tradition and gives it continued life. During festivals God releases us from daily patterns of life and the truncated vision of existence which accompanies it. We readily acknowledge that God has revealed himself in the Christian and Jewish traditions and so is responsible for their existence. In a complementary way we, the believers who hand on the tradition about God, keep God in existence within society, for God is known only through spoken and practiced religious traditions.

Both Judaism and Christianity depend on Passover as a central symbol of God's care for them. A review of the history and development of Passover is a glimpse into the substance of both Judaism and Christianity. Passover manifests the beliefs and attitudes which give vitality to both traditions and enables them to survive. It also expresses the enjoyment of God's people in his presence. This book attempts to present and explain the symbolic center of both traditions and to show the deep relationship which permanently binds Judaism and Christianity to one another, just as Jesus, who reigns as Lord of all, remains a Jew, bound to his people and century.

Many Christians know vaguely that Christianity arose from Judaism and that Jesus and his early followers were Jews. Yet, today Christians and Jews belong to two separate communities which worship and live independently. Both groups think of themselves as different and imagine it was always that way. Yet, Jesus was a first century Jew who celebrated Passover along with his fellow Jews. Though the celebration of Passover had changed from the early days of the Israelite kings, the feast with its songs, symbols and stories had remained recognizably the same. When Jesus prayed and celebrated

Passover, he taught a small group of followers about the Kingdom of God. After Jesus died his followers recognized that he had risen from the dead and soon they began to speak of him as the Passover lamb. Passover became a celebration of Jesus' death and resurrection and the community of believers replaced Israel as the saved community. The "history" of what happened at Passover was broadened to include the salvation of all believers.

To understand Jesus and Passover, we must first understand Passover in Judaism: how it began, what it meant, how it developed and what it is today. Then the faith of the early Christians, that God does in Jesus what had been done in Egypt, will take on concrete meaning and force. The words, images, symbols and actions we use in worship and teaching die if we fail to understand how Jesus' actions and words were built upon the history and faith of Israel. God did not send a superhuman figure into the world to dazzle everyone who saw and heard him; God became a human in a small country with its own language, ideas, traditions, and religion. Only through that religion and its attendent culture can Jesus and his early followers speak to us in the twentieth century.

Passover began as a festival among shepherds long before the Hebrew people existed and it endures as a religious celebration within the family and in the synagogue today. Transformed by Christians it lives another life as a celebration and explanation of the salvation brought to humans by Jesus. The chapters of this book will follow the development of this central feast in both Judaism and Christianity. Millennia ago the Passover sacrifice sought the gods' protection for the herds as they traveled from winter to summer pastures. Human awareness of the need for the help of the divine underlies the celebration of Passover in every century. When the Israelites adopted Passover as a central festival, they looked to their primeval experience of salvation from slavery in Egypt. Their very lives and identity as a nation required safety and security. When the Temple was built in the tenth century B.C., Israel celebrated Passover in that magnificent setting with solemn ritual and song as a national feast.

Jesus participated in the Temple worship, in the excitement of the thousands who crowded Jerusalem, in the rigors of the pilgrimage to the holy city and in the raw, direct symbolism of animal sacrifice. After the destruction of the Temple by the Romans in 70 A.D. Jews moved the Passover celebration from the holy city to every Jewish home. In place of the lamb, which could no longer be slaughtered at the Temple, unleavened bread and bitter herbs became the ritual center of the meal.

During the first and second centuries the early Christian believers adopted much of the Passover tradition and transformed it into an explanation and celebration of what Jesus had done by dying and rising for us. Salvation as an abstract word cries out for content. Salvation from sin lacks the clarity and drama of the exodus from Egypt. God's historical care for Israel exemplifies his battle against evil and gives concrete meaning to Jesus' victory over evil.

Passover must not be cherished like an heirloom. Christians who eat the Christian Passover meal, Jesus' body and blood, must live in a way worthy of Jesus, God and Passover. Various Christian writers have appealed to Passover as a motive for sinlessness, a sign of closeness to God, a model for perseverance in faith and a symbol of hope for final redemption. Passover lives on in both the Jewish and Christian communities as a central ritual which expresses diversely each community's identity and nature. In Passover we meet Judaism and Christianity at their core, the same and yet different. Most importantly, we meet the God who has communicated with humans and who lives in community with his creatures.

# 2

# *The Origins of Passover*

Readers of the Bible first learn of the feast of Passover in the Book of Exodus, chapter 11. The Hebrews are about to be freed from Egypt, but to effect this escape God brings one last punishment on the Egyptians, the death of their first-born children and animals. God gives the Hebrews specific instructions on how to avoid having their own first-born children killed along with the Egyptians'. They are to kill a lamb or goat and put the blood on their door posts so that God will pass over them without harm. The feast of Passover is a memorial of this last great night in Egypt when the Hebrews were freed from slavery.

The story is central to Judaism because the Hebrews became a people when God led them out of Egypt. When reading the simple story of Passover night in Exodus, chapters 12 and 13, one notices some remarkable details. First, the narrative of Israel's confrontation with the Egyptians is interrupted by a series of instructions given by God to Moses concerning future Passover celebrations. Besides narrating the events taking place in Egypt, the author of Exodus instructs his Jewish readers on how to celebrate the Passover *now*. The past and present are joined in a unique way at Passover.

Three separate practices are explained in chapters 12 and 13: the Passover sacrifice, the feast of Unleavened Bread and the consecration of the first-born. The sacrifice of the Passover animal and the meal following this sacrifice is the best known of the three. Secondly, detailed and separate instructions are given for the eating of unleavened bread for the week after Passover. This observance is called the feast of the Unleavened Bread. Fi-

5

nally, the command to consecrate all first-born animals and children to God by sacrificing or redeeming the animals and redeeming the children is appended to the instructions for the Passover sacrifice and the eating of unleavened bread.

These three observances, the Passover sacrifice, the eating of unleavened bread and the consecration of the first-born to God, were originally separate from one another and unrelated to the escape of the Hebrews from slavery in Egypt. Almost certainly the two festivals and the consecration of the first-born were pre-Israelite practices carried on by many tribes and peoples in the Middle East. All are related to the spring (the time of Passover) when crops are harvested and animals bring forth their young. These early fertility practices were adopted by Israel, integrated into its own experience in Egypt, and used in the worship of its God, Yahweh.

*Pre-Israelite Passover*

In order to understand the meaning of Passover in the Old Testament and then the use made of it in the New Testament we must first examine the underlying symbolism and rationale of each practice associated with Passover. All the practices spring from the agricultural calendar of the Middle East. Winter is the only time of rain, so it is then that planting is done. A few weeks later, in spring, the harvests begin. The feasts of Passover and Unleavened Bread are celebrated near the spring solstice in March or April. The feast of Unleavened Bread and the offering of the first sheaf harvested during that week celebrate the beginning of the barley harvest. Several weeks later, in June, Pentecost marks the end of the wheat and grain harvest. Finally, the grape, olive and fruit harvests occasion the feast of Booths in the fall (September) along with the new year festival. This agricultural structure persists to the present in the Jewish calendar as well as in the Christian liturgical calendar.

The Passover sacrifice began as a spring practice of herdsmen. During the colder months of winter they moved their herds to warm, low pastures where the young would be born. In the spring these semi-nomadic people would move higher in the mountains to summer pastures which were cooler for their herds and provided better grazing. The journey between pastures was dangerous for the herds, especially for the recently born young who had to keep up or be lost. The sacrifice of one of the young lambs or goats symbolized the dangers to be avoided and recognized the necessity for divine protection for humans and beasts on the journey. The help of the gods would save the flocks from imminent dangers. Note that the Passover sacrifice is concerned with travel and safety, a concern of Israel as it leaves Egypt. The symbolism of the feast could sustain a wide range of meaning and was eventually adapted to the experience of sedentary Israelites.

The feast of Unleavened Bread requires that people rid their dwelling or camp of all old leavened bread and all old leaven. For a week they eat dough which has not been leavened as a sign that the old is finished and the new about to begin. This celebration arose among settled agricultural people. It marks the beginning of the harvest season and recognizes the dependence of humans on God for the fertility of the earth which feeds and gives life. Unleavened bread is often eaten in the Middle East among nomads and settled folk alike, but its exclusive use during a special period takes on symbolic depth. In the story of the flight from Egypt the lack of leaven is attributed to the haste with which Israel left Egypt, but it also retains its metaphoric reference to beginning life anew.

The obligation to sacrifice first-born animals to God and redeem first-born children by a gift to God arose among people who raised herds, just as the command to offer first-fruits of new trees (Dt 26:5–11) arose among agricultural people. The gift of the first-born to God recognizes God as the giver of life in the mysterious process of conception and asks his continued protection and cooperation in the natural fertility so necessary for life. The blood of the sacrifice of first-born animals is linked to the blood of the Passover sacrifice which protected the lives of the Hebrew first-born in Egypt while the Egyptian first-born were destroyed.

These three spring practices, the Passover sacrifice, the eating of unleavened bread and the sacrifice or redemption of the first-born, express deeply felt needs for the protection of life. They acknowledge that God is the giver and protector of life and that without his help life itself is in danger. Given the fundamental human realities symbolized by these practices, they were easily linked to the concrete historical experience of Israel. Israel came into being as a nation when God saved it from slavery in Egypt, protected it in the wilderness when it was in danger and gave it a land "flowing with milk and honey," that is, a land which could sustain life and provide security. God's life-giving action in spring and God's life-saving action in Egypt merge smoothly in the Jewish feast of Passover/Unleavened Bread.

*Passover in Israel*

The many texts in the Old Testament which speak of Passover fail to tell us exactly how this festival developed, when and where it was celebrated and what it meant originally. Our account of the pre-Israelite origin of Passover has been drawn from hints in the Old Testament and from what we know of other religions in the area. Many gaps remain to be filled. We shall look at the most important places in the Old Testament which speak of Passover and try to understand its meaning and its probable development through the centuries. In this way we will comprehend more clearly the kind of feast which Jesus celebrated at the time he died and rose and the meaning which it gives to Jesus' sacrifice.

The story of the first Passover in Exodus 12 and 13 contains not only an account of the events which took place in Egypt but also instructions for celebrating Passover, the feast of Unleavened Bread and the consecration of the first-born. Chapter 12 interrupts the narrative with the instruction: "This month shall be for you the beginning of months; it shall be the first month of the year for you. Tell all the congregation of Israel that on the tenth day of this month they shall take every man a lamb. . . ." Because Passover is so important, the month in which it is celebrated will be the first month of the year. The traditional Middle Eastern year began in the fall and this is when Jews celebrate their religious new year today. When Israel came under Babylonian influence in the seventh and sixth centuries B.C., the later Babylonian custom of observing the new year in the spring was adopted. The biblical writers connected the new first month of the year with Passover and the deliverance from Egypt. That the organization of the calendar is taken up in the middle of the Exodus story shows that the author has the present and future on his mind as well as the past. He sees all of Israelite life bound up with the past, especially with this most important of events, the saving of Israel from slavery in Egypt.

The description of the Passover meal in Exodus 12:1–13 both describes what the Hebrews did in Egypt and gives instructions for the recreating of that meal in later generations. The Passover lamb is sacrificed on the fourteenth day of the month, which is the full moon. It is eaten by family groups large enough to consume the lamb completely, and if anything remains, it must be burned before morning. The lamb must be roasted, not boiled in the usual manner. Blood from the lamb must be put on the doorposts and lintel. The participants in the meal must leave their belts and sandals on, have their staffs in hand, and eat in haste; in sum they must be ready to travel.

A second account of the Passover meal makes its purpose more explicit:

> You shall observe this rite as an ordinance for you and for your sons for ever. And when you come to the land which the Lord will give you, as he has promised, you shall keep this service. And when your children say to you, 'What do you mean by this service?' you shall say, 'It is the sacrifice of the Lord's Passover, for he passed over the houses of the people of Israel in Egypt ... (Ex 12:21–27).

In the author's mind the events in Egypt and the present situation of Israel celebrating Passover cannot be separated from one another. He is so comfortable with the close relationship of past and present that he intertwines ritual instructions with the dramatic account of the escape from Egypt.

## Instructions for Passover

Exodus 12 and 13 contain several accounts of Passover and the rituals associated with it. Without going into excessive detail we shall review the main points, which will recur in succeeding chapters when we deal with Passover at the time of Jesus. As we just noted, at the beginning of chapter 12 Israel is commanded to eat each lamb within a group which is big enough to consume the lamb, even if it means combining households. The whole lamb must be consumed during the night or, since it is consecrated for special use, the remainder must be burned. The lamb must be a year old, which probably does not mean a new-born lamb, but an animal less than a year old and large enough to feed a family. The animal is killed in the evening, outside the door of the house or tent. The Passover sacrifice was not originally a Temple sacrifice, but an act of family worship. The animal is not boiled in a pot in the normal manner, but roasted on a spit over the fire.

This latter custom derives from nomads who had no room to carry pots on their pack animals.

The second account of Passover in 12:21–27 adds a couple of details. The blood of the sacrificed animal is to be caught in a basin and then smeared on the doorposts and lintel using a bunch of hyssop (a small bush of the Middle East). Further regulations for participation in the Passover meal are given in 12:43–49. No foreigners may eat of the sacrificial meal; aliens who reside in Israel and who have been circumcised may participate. The lamb must be eaten in one house and the meat may not be carried to another house. In addition, the bones of the animal may not be broken. This last regulation is quoted in John's passion account (19:36) as a prophecy of Jesus' death.

To summarize, Exodus 12 and 13 give commands concerning the eating of unleavened bread in two places, 12:14–20 and 13:3–10, and regulations for the consecration of the first-born of animals and humans near the conclusion of chapter 13. All three practices, the Passover sacrifice, the unleavened bread and the consecration of the first-born, are connected by the Old Testament editor to the escape of Israel from Egypt. The separate regulations for each practice and the independent internal coherence of each mode of worship shows that these feasts and practices were not originally connected to the exodus from Egypt, but that they have been adapted to fit new circumstances and needs in Israel. In each case the editor has framed similar instructions which tell the Israelites to keep the practice when they come into the land which the Lord will give them and further command them to teach their children what God did for them when the children ask why these practices are kept. For example:

> You shall observe this rite as an ordinance for you and for your sons for ever. And when you come to the land which the Lord will give you, as he has promised, you shall keep this service. And when your children say to you, "What do you mean by this service?" you shall say, "It is the sacrifice of the Lord's passover, for he passed over the houses of the people of Israel in Egypt, when he slew the Egyptians but spared our houses" (Ex 12:24–27; see also 13:8–10; 13:14–16).

These instructions and explanations explain the centrality and importance of Passover in Jewish worship.

*Passover During the Monarchy*

We do not know for certain how Passover was celebrated during the time of the kings of Israel and Judah (1000—600 B.C.). The Book of Exodus contains two old calendars of festivals which are to be observed. Passover and the feast of Unleavened Bread are separate in those calendars. Three of the feasts on those calendars, the feasts of Unleavened Bread, Weeks and Booths, are designated pilgrimage feasts (Ex 23:14–17). But this passage does not mention the Passover sacrifice or meal in connection with the feast of Unleavened Bread. On these three agricultural feasts all males are required to "appear before the Lord God." Late in the monarchy making a pilgrimage to appear before the Lord means going to the Temple in Jerusalem. But early in the settlement of Israel the command refers to worship at various local holy places which were traditional tribal meeting places where sacrifice was offered.

Another old calendar of feasts (Ex 34:18–26) refers to the same three pilgrimage feasts and then at the end gives a specific regulation concerning Passover without saying exactly when it is observed or directly connecting it with the feast of Unleavened Bread: "You shall not offer the blood of my sacrifice with leaven; neither shall the sacrifice of the feast of the Passover be left until morning." Sacrifice in general and unleavened bread are mentioned and the eating of the Passover lamb during the evening and night is presumed, but little precise information is given.

During the early Israelite period and on into the monarchy we are not sure whether the Passover sacrifice was carried out at each person's home or at community shrines. Since the description of the feast of Passover in Exodus presumes a home setting and since the Passover sacrifice is not explicitly connected with "appearing before the Lord God" at one of his shrines, Passover was probably a local, family celebration.

The Book of Deuteronomy contains old traditions which the author has modified and edited to fit a reform program carried out in the seventh century B.C. The author wished to safeguard monotheism and suppress worship of gods other than Yahweh by centralizing all animal sacrifice and agricultural offerings in one place, the Temple in Jerusalem. Probably the core of the book was available to King Josiah of Judah when he reformed Israelite worship in the seventh century. The Book of Deuteronomy reached its final form during the exile in the sixth century. Its radical reform of Israelite worship, which meant the destruction of hundreds of local altars and holy sites, did not succeed completely, and until the Temple was destroyed a few decades after Josiah, many Israelites continued to celebrate feasts locally. Those who were influenced by the Deuteronomic reform would have begun traveling up to Jerusalem to sacrifice the Passover lamb and offer the sacrifices appropriate to the feast of Unleavend Bread. This reformed practice prevailed in Judaism when the Temple was rebuilt and was the custom during the first century A.D. when Jesus lived.

Deuteronomy 16:1–8 speaks of both the Passover sacrifice and the feast of Unleavened Bread. For the first time the Passover sacrifice and the eating of unleavened bread for seven days are intimately linked with one another. But even here some awkward transitions in the passage suggest that originally the regulations for the two observances were separate. For example, 16:7 says that the morning after the Passover meal the worshipers are to return to their tents. But they are also expected to be at the central shrine for a solemn assembly on the last day of the eight-day festival of Unleavened Bread (16:8). The stress on worship at the Temple can be seen in two unique regulations for the Passover sacrifice which were not followed in later times, but which are consistent with sacrifices at a temple rather than at home. Deuteronomy says that the animal may be drawn from the flock or the *herd*. The flock includes goats and lambs, the traditional Passover animals mentioned in Exodus. The herd includes oxen, which were sacrificed at the Temple, but not at Passover. Secondly, Exodus says clearly that the animal must be roasted, not boiled (the normal mode of cooking). Deuteronomy says the opposite, probably because sacrifices cooked and eaten in the Temple were normally boiled.

The regulations for celebrating Passover scattered throughout the early books of the Bible vary somewhat and show signs of development. The later dominance of the Temple, the reform of Josiah and the regularizing of feasts which went on during the exile all had an effect on Passover and contributed to its form in the first century when early Christians modified its rituals and symbolism to express their faith in Jesus. Further insight into Passover can be gained by looking at the Passover celebrations recorded in the Hebrew Bible and evaluating their importance and meaning to Israel.

### Passover's Importance

When the Passover celebration is mentioned in the Bible, it is usually as a crucially important feast with major significance for Israel. For example, in the Book of Joshua, chapter 5, when Israel crosses the Jordan River and enters the promised land, the people gather at an ancient sanctuary, Gilgal. There those born during the wandering in the wilderness were circumcised. Then the people celebrated the Passover and on the next day ate of the produce of the land. Passover reminded the people of how God saved them from Egypt and gave them this land. It also served as a ritual transition from wandering to residence in the land which they had been promised.

Centuries later during the 600's B.C. King Josiah of Judah initiated a reform of Judaism. Many Israelites were worshiping gods other than Yahweh and engaging in practices abhorrent to God's law. The discovery of a law book in the Temple (perhaps the core of the Book of Deuteronomy) prompted many leaders and people to repent and do away with temples and sanctuaries where other gods were worshiped. At the climax of this reform, called the Deuteronomic reform, the king commanded the people, "Keep the Passover to the Lord your God, as it is written in the book of the covenant." (2 Kgs 23:21) The biblical author continues: "For no such Passover had been kept since the days of the judges who judged Israel, or during all the days of the kings of Israel or of the kings of Judah; but in the eighteenth year of King Josiah this Passover was kept in Jerusalem." What the author probably means by Passover is keeping the Passover in Jerusalem and celebrating it as a nation, the way the people did at Gilgal with Joshua. In the interim people had celebrated Passover in their homes or at local shrines, but now Josiah had done away with local celebrations and centralized worship at Jerusalem, a change the biblical author heartily approves of. Celebration of Passover symbolizes and climaxes the return to faithful worship of Yahweh, Israel's God.

In 587 B.C. the Babylonians conquered Jerusalem and destroyed both the city and the Temple. The priests, royal family and other leaders of Israel were transported across the desert to Babylon to live in exile. The bulk of the farmers were left in Judea without leadership, national identity or organized worship. In Babylon, the prophet Ezekiel quotes a series of regulations for keeping proper festivals when the Temple is restored. The leaders of Judaism in the exile were anxious to gather together Jewish teachings and keep them in existence even though their country and Temple had been destroyed. Concerning Passover he says: "In the first month, on the fourteenth day of the month, you shall celebrate the feast of the Passover, and for seven days unleavened bread shall be eaten" (Ez 45:21). This is the first text in which Passover and the feast of the Unleavened Bread are originally and smoothly joined to one another. It was probably during the exile or just before it that the two feasts began to merge into one.

Fifty years after the destruction of the Temple Cyrus the Persian conquered the Babylonian Empire and in an attempt to win the hearts of his many new subjects he allowed the Jewish exiles to return to Judea and rebuild the Temple. Only some of the priests and leaders returned, and even then it took them over twenty years to complete the rebuilding of the Temple against local opposition.

When the Temple was finally completed and dedicated, the first feast celebrated there was Passover. For the returned exiles Passover was the most important feast and its symbolism most appropriate to their own experience of being saved by God from captivity. The Book of Ezra recounts the joyful feast and connects it firmly with the feast of Unleavened Bread, just as it is today.

On the fourteenth day of the first month the returned exiles kept the Passover. For the priests and the Levites had purified themselves together; all of them were clean. So they killed the Passover lamb for all the returned exiles, for their fellow priests and for themselves; it was eaten by the people of Israel who had returned from exile, and also by everyone who had joined them, and separated himself from the pollutions of the peoples of the land to worship the Lord, the God of Israel. And they kept the feast of unleavened bread seven days with joy; for the Lord had made them joyful, and had turned the heart of the king of Assyria to them, so that he aided them in the work of the house of God, the God of Israel (Ezr 6:19–22).

The Passover sacrifice was conducted in the Temple under the supervision of the priests and Levites, a practice that continued all through the second Temple period including the time of Jesus. The sacrifice and the following seven-day feast of Unleavened Bread are experienced as times of joy and of the highest importance for the community. Passover has become the premier feast of the Jewish calendar.

Passover went through a long evolution from a spring feast of semi-nomads to an Israelite family and clan memorial of the deliverance from Egypt. With the dominance of the Temple it became a solemn sacrifice in Jerusalem. Later in the reorganization of Temple worship which followed the destruction of the Temple and its rebuilding, Passover became the first and most important day of the week-long feast of Unleavened Bread and eventually its name was used for both feasts. As the centuries passed and the celebration developed, Passover became the most beloved and central feast in the Jewish calendar (with the Day of Atonement in the fall being its only rival).

# 3

# *Passover During Jesus' Lifetime*

In the first century when Jesus lived, the Passover sacrifice and meal was celebrated only in Jerusalem because the animal eaten at the meal (a lamb or a goat) had to be slaughtered in the Temple. Jewish practice was regulated by the Book of Deuteronomy which moved major festivals to Jerusalem and forbade the original local celebrations. "Three times a year all your males shall appear before the Lord your God at the place which he will choose: at the feast of Unleavened Bread, at the feast of Weeks, and at the feast of Booths" (Dt 16:16). These three feasts were called pilgrimage festivals because large crowds of men, women and children ascended to Jerusalem and the Temple to celebrate them. The excitement and confusion of these journeys are reflected in the story of Jesus' trip to Jerusalem with his parents when he was twelve. "Now his parents went to Jerusalem every year at the feast of the Passover. And when he was twelve years old, they went up according to custom; and when the feast was ended, as they were returning, the boy Jesus stayed behind in Jerusalem. His parents did not know it, but supposing him to be in the company they went a day's journey, and they sought him among their kinfolk and acquaintances" (Lk 2:41–44). Many people traveled in large groups each year. When boys reached puberty, twelve to thirteen years of age, they too were required to keep the commandment to journey to Jerusalem for the festivals. Pilgrimages remove people from their ordinary place and daily routine and bring them to meet

God in the sacred time and place. Naturally, they produce awe, excitement, fear, reflection and uncertainty. The stress and unfamiliarity of the journey and surroundings mirror the emotions felt when in contact with God who is holy and different. The emphasis on celebrating the Passover by pilgrimage suggests its importance to Judaism and explains its influence on the Christian feast of Easter which commemorates Jesus' journey to Jerusalem and then to death and resurrected life.

At Passover pilgrims filled every available room in Jerusalem and set up tents near the Temple. Lodgings were most important at Passover because observance of the festival required a place for a communal Passover meal within Jerusalem. The Gospel according to Mark recounts Jesus' search for a room in which to eat the Passover meal: "On the first day of Unleavened Bread, when they sacrificed the Passover lamb, his disciples said to him, 'Where will you have us go and prepare for you to eat the Passover?'" Jesus tells two disciples to follow a man carrying a water jar "and wherever he enters, say to the householder, 'The Teacher says, Where is my guest room where I am to eat the Passover with my disciples?'" (14:12–14). Jesus and his disciples faced the common anxiety associated with finding a room in Jerusalem in which to eat the Passover meal.

Jerusalem was the religious and political center of Judaism, the largest city in the area and even more importantly the sacred, symbolic home of Judaism. Though Jerusalem and the Holy Land are special to Christians, they are necessary to Jews. The city had been rebuilt and expanded in stages since its destruction by the Babylonians several centuries previously in 587 B.C. Just before the time of Jesus, Herod the Great, infamous for brutal family intrigues and political repression, had expanded the walls of Jerusalem, doubled the size of the Temple enclosure, beautified the Temple building, and built porticoes, monumental stairways, streets and a fortified palace for himself. Jerusalem became a major city of the Eastern Roman Empire and its effect on pilgrims was expressed by Jesus' disciples as they left the Temple just before his death: "Look, Teacher, what wonderful stones and what wonderful buildings!" (Mk 13:1).

Jerusalem rests on the mountain spine of Palestine and is built on two ridges running north–south with a valley between them. The Temple compound covered the northern end of the eastern ridge; it was surrounded by a wall which marked off the sacred area and also constituted part of the

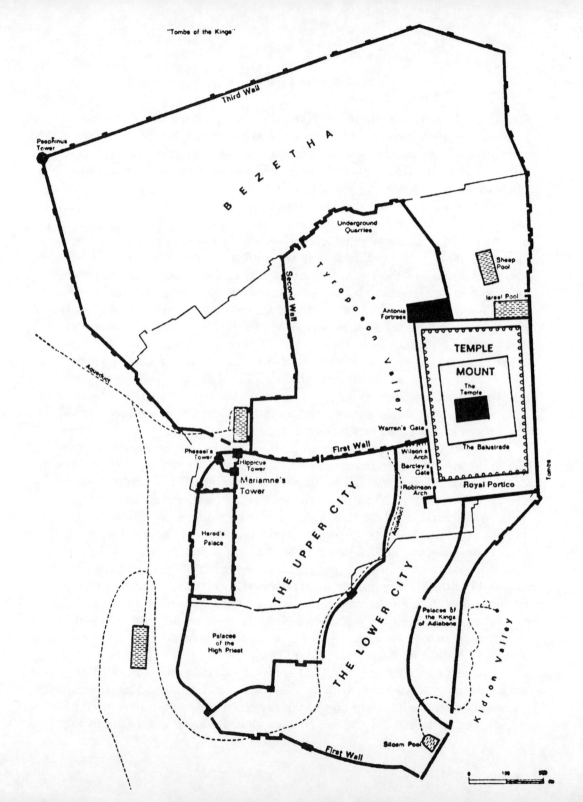

"Tombs of the Kings"

Third Wall

B E Z E T H A

Psephinus Tower

Underground Quarries

Sheep Pool

Israel Pool

T y r o p o e o n   V a l l e y

Second Wall

Aqueduct

Antonia Fortress

TEMPLE

MOUNT

The Temple

The Balustrade

Warren's Gate

Phasael's Tower

Hippicus Tower

Mariamne's Tower

First Wall

Wilson's Arch

Barclay's Gate

Robinson Arch

Royal Portico

Tombs

Herod's Palace

THE UPPER CITY

Aqueduct

THE LOWER CITY

Palaces of the Kings of Adiabene

Palaces of the High Priest

Kidron Valley

First Wall

Siloam Pool

100   200

city's defense system. In addition, both ridges and the Tyropoeon Valley between were surrounded by a wall which ran along the brow of the Kidron
Valley to the east and the Hinnom Valley to the south and west. To the
north the wall was on flat land approaching the city; consequently this was
the direction used for attack by armies besieging Jerusalem.

Jerusalem was densely settled within its walls. Archeological excava-
tions have uncovered a wide variety of houses, from large, luxurious man-
sions on the western hill to small, plainer dwellings on the slopes.
Population in antiquity is notoriously difficult to estimate and figures given
by ancient authors are usually exaggerated. A conservative estimate for the
population of Jerusalem is 50,000. During Passover visitors probably num-
bered an additional 100,000 or even more. The interior of the city was
marked off by defensive walls along both brows of the Tyropoeon Valley
which ran down the center of the city. The western side was dominated by
Herod's palace with its three huge defensive towers. To the east the Temple
with its fortified enclosure and high walls awed all who entered. Most
houses and courtyards were small and humble; streets were narrow and
wound around the contours of the hills and valleys. Pools, aqueducts, broad
streets and stairways down into the valleys dotted the city.

## The Temple

When the Temple was built on the top of a narrow ridge, the area
around it was limited by the steep hillsides. Herod in the first century B.C.
doubled the size of the Temple enclosure by building massive retaining
walls and filling them in to create a large level area. The foundations of
Herod's wall still stand two thousand years later. The southern portion of
the western wall (between Wilson's and Robinson's Arches on the map) has
been a place of prayer for Jews since shortly after the destruction of Jerusalem in 70 A.D. It is called the "Wailing Wall" because here Jews mourned
the loss of the Temple and the destruction of Jerusalem by the Romans.
Even today it is the most revered site in Israel for Jews. The wall was built
on bedrock, using stones three to ten feet long and four feet high, carefully
laid one on another and decorated with smooth margins and raised surfaces.

Because the Temple area was raised and walled, it had to be ap-

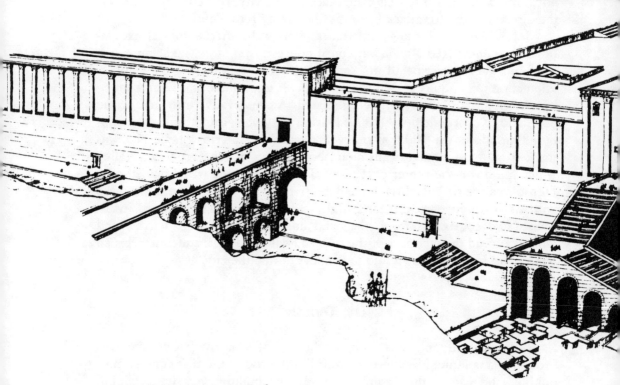

*Temple—Herodian Period*

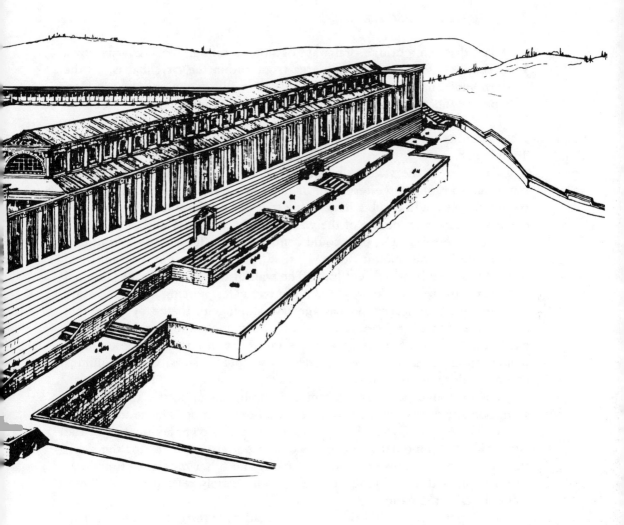

proached through a bridge, stairways or sloping tunnels, each guarded by a gate. People entered the Temple area from within the city, that is, on the western and southern sides. From the western hill of the city, where Herod's palace and the houses of the rich were, worshipers could proceed toward the Temple along a broad street and cross the Tyropoeon Valley on an arched bridge (Wilson's Arch on the map) that brought the road into the Temple enclosure.

For those in the valley a broad, paved road with sculpted decorations ran at the foot of the western wall of the Temple mount. At the southwest corner people could climb a huge stone stairway up the side of the wall to a covered walkway at the top of the wall. (See the sketch of the southern end of the Temple Area.) Or, they could continue to the left along the southern side of the Temple mount down a broad, paved road into a large, open square over five hundred feet long. The wall of the Temple mount loomed above this square and stairways led up to two gates piercing the wall. Inside the gates were underground passageways sloping up to the open Temple area above. The stairs leading to the gate on the left, the double or Hulda gate, are about two hundred feet wide and thirty in number. These monumental public areas were decorated with sculpted friezes, Greek columns and other decorative details.

Underground passageways conducting pilgrims up to the Temple area, storerooms, cisterns, pools, and aqueducts honeycombed the southern end of the Temple enclosure. The Temple mount was a complex quarter of the city which accommodated not only worship but also supplies for the sacrifices and priests, defensive needs of the city and other municipal functions. The Temple with its religious festivals was intimately related to the society and politics of the nation.

The open area around the Temple spread over thirty-five acres. On all four sides of this open space were porticoes, which are covered walkways. They were about fifty feet wide with roofs supported by rows of huge Greek columns. In these covered porticoes courts met, teachers instructed their students and merchants carried on business. The range of activities carried on here can be seen in the use Jesus made of the Temple. "About the middle of the feast (of Tabernacles) Jesus went up into the temple and taught" (Jn 7:14). "Jesus sat down opposite the treasury, and watched the multitude putting money into the treasury" (Mk 12:41). John notes that Jesus was walking in Solomon's Portico (the one on the east) when a group of Jews gathered around him to ask him if he was the Messiah (10:22–24). The Acts of the Apostles records that the early believers in Jesus met regularly in Solomon's Portico (Acts 5:12).

Jesus' objections to some of the activities during Passover are dramatized in John:

> The Passover of the Jews was at hand and Jesus went up to Jerusalem. In the temple he found those who were selling oxen and sheep and pigeons, and the money-changers at their business. And making a whip of cords, he drove them all, with the sheep and oxen, out of the temple; and he poured out the coins of the money-changers, and overturned their tables. And he told those who sold pigeons, 'Take these things away; you shall not make my Father's house a house of trade' " (Jn 2:13–16).

Despite Jesus' objection to the merchants in the Temple, numerous secular activities were normal and needed to make the Temple function. The Temple was part of the city and nation and intimately linked to all its activities. The Western vision of a church (or synagogue) as a quiet place reserved for certain rituals and characterized by proper demeanor is foreign to the ancient Near East.

In the center of the thirty-five acre raised enclosure stood the Temple with its sacred courts and buildings. The Temple was not a single building, like a church or synagogue today, but a group of buildings and courtyards clearly marked off and raised one above the other. The inner most holy place, the holy of holies, was a room thirty-three feet square and thirty-three feet high, which was entered only once a year by the high priest on the Day of Atonement. Priests could enter the area around the most holy place; male Jews were kept back from the Temple building and altar and female Jews one court farther away. Gentiles could enter none of the complex of buildings and courtyards surrounding the Temple, but were separated from the sacred buildings by the "balustrade," a five foot high wall of stone latticework. At each opening in this barrier was a sign in Greek and Latin, the two international languages of the day, warning that non-Jews who entered would be put to death.

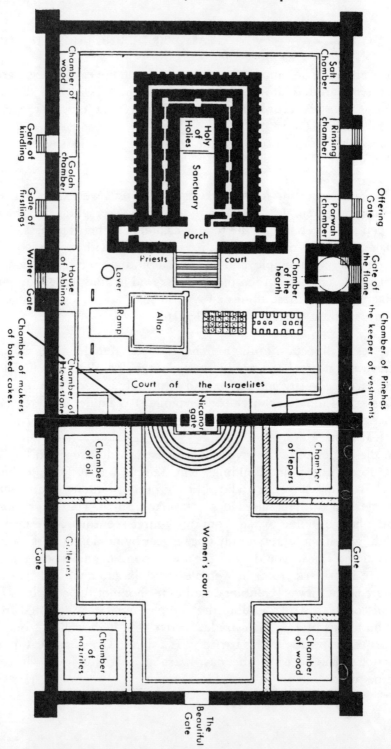

The sacred area within the balustrade, according to one report, was almost three hundred yards square. Much of our information comes from the Jewish legal collection called the Mishna. Though it was composed over a century after the destruction of the Temple, it probably gives us a reasonably accurate picture of the Temple and its precincts. Within the balustrade was a huge retaining wall sixty-six feet high backed by an embankment twenty-three feet wide. This wall raised the Temple buildings above the rest of the compound and also provided a last line of defense in war. Within this wall the Temple stood at the western end with its door facing east. Consequently, worshipers entered at the eastern end of the compound, opposite the door, and proceeded through a series of courtyards toward the Temple.

Approaching from the east a Jew walked through the "Beautiful Gate" into the Courtyard of Women, a large open space beyond which women could not pass. People entering this courtyard could look west and see the facade of the Temple at the other end of the sacred area. At the western end of the Courtyard of Women male worshipers could continue up a semi-circular bank of fifteen stairs to the Nicanor Gate whose doors were plated with beautifully wrought copper. On these stairs the Levites stood to play their instruments and sing during worship.

Once through the Nicanor Gate the worshiper had entered the inner court, an area with yet another high wall around it. Non-priests were required to remain in the Courtyard of the Israelites, a narrow strip just inside the Nicanor Gate, which was only nineteen feet deep, but ran the whole width of the inner court, 222 feet. Here the Passover animals were sacrificed by the heads of households present in Jerusalem for the feast. All other sacrifices and sacred rituals were carried out by the priests in the area reserved for them slightly above and beyond the Courtyard of the Israelites.

As a Jew looked up toward the Temple he saw to the left of its entrance a large altar on a raised platform. Here all sacrificial portions of the animals were burned. To the right of the Temple entrance was a group of tables, posts and hooks set up for slaughtering and cleaning the animals offered in the Temple. Activity in the Temple differed strikingly from the quiet prayer and propriety of modern Jewish and Christian congregations. Live animals had to be herded near the Temple, with the attendant noise and smell. Priests were engaged in killing the animals and butchering the carcasses, an activity kept discretely behind the scenes in modern commerce, not to speak of religion.

Nearer the Temple entrance, on the left, was a huge container for water, used in ritual purification of the priests engaged in sacred activities. Surrounding the Temple was a three story building containing numerous rooms for storage and preparation. Under the Temple site both then and now are a series of passageways to cisterns and pools probably used for purification. The priests and Levites could enter the Temple area only if they were ritually pure. Ritual purity, unfamiliar to modern Westerners, has little to do with hygiene. Rather, a participant must prepare himself to approach God by following prescribed and detailed rituals that separate him from anything which might impede communion with God. Certain kinds of animals and food, human corpses, sexual activity and numerous other things rendered one unclean. These things and activities were not seen as evil or morally wrong in themselves, only as an obstacle to direct and proper contact with God. One who had contact with these things had to purify himself in prescribed ways during set periods of waiting before resuming his normal duties.

The entrance to the Temple building dominated and overshadowed the Courtyard of the Israelites and the sacrifices of the priests. The vestibule or porch to the Temple building was twelve steps higher than the courtyard where the priests worked. It was 175 feet from left to right and seventy feet high with columns and other sculpted architectural features decorating its facade. Its open portal was veiled with curtains. Through this antechamber priests entered the next room, the sanctuary, and other rooms off to the sides which were intimately connected with Temple worship.

The sanctuary, the second room of the Temple, was entered from the vestibule through a pair of gold plated doors whose opening was covered by a curtain. Within the sanctuary, the walls were covered with gold decorations and gold plate as were all the ritual furnishings. The room was lighted by the menorah, the familiar seven branched candlestick. In the middle of the room was a small gold altar on which incense was offered twice daily; coals were brought in from the altar of sacrifice outside and incense was thrown on them. In this room twelve loaves of bread (the bread of the presence) were laid out on a table weekly. These offerings symbolized Israel's dependence on God for food and life itself. Entrance to the sanctuary was restricted to priests so that the ordinary Israelite could not even view the sacred rituals. The God of Israel was conceived of as holy and separate from everyday activities. The many rules for priestly activity ensured a lively sense of reverence.

The holy of holies, reached by a ramp at the far end of the sanctuary, was incalculably more inaccessible than the other parts of the Temple. A curtain separated this windowless thirty-three foot cube chamber from the view of all, even the priests. Only on the Day of Atonement (Yom Kippur) could the high priest enter this room alone to offer incense. In the period after the destruction of the first Temple by the Babylonians the holy of holies was empty. The ark of the covenant and the cherubim, the holiest objects associated with Israelite religion, had been housed in the holy of holies, but when the Babylonians destroyed the Temple they were either destroyed or carried away as booty and lost. This loss was not crucial because Jews did not depend on an image of their God. The ark was a holy object from the desert days and the cherubim, a pair of winged beasts with human heads, were traditional guardians of holy places. God's presence was conceived of as present above the cherubim and the ark, not as in them. The Temple and its most sacred room symbolized and provided sacred space for God's presence on earth among his people.

The Temple and its enclosure inspired excitement and reverence in both Jew and Gentile who visited. From the massive walls surrounding the Temple mount to the simplicity of an empty sacred room, from the crowds and commerce of the porticoes to the silently burning incense offered daily, the Temple was the center and climax of Jewish religious belief and worship and at the same time separate and different from anything directly experienced by the individual believer. The Temple stood as a fitting symbol of God and God's complex relationship with his creatures.


## Temple Worship

Public prayer and sacrifice in the Temple required the labor of numerous priests and Levites. Levites at the time of Jesus were a lower class of priest entrusted with keeping order in the Temple, providing for physical necessities and leading the singing with voice and instrument. Central moments in Temple worship were announced by trumpet blasts, and the daily sacrifices, offered morning and evening on behalf of the whole people, were accompanied by music and the singing of psalms. During the day private sacrifices, as required or urged by the Bible, were brought by the people and offered by the priests. When animals were offered, they most frequently were not burned whole on the altar. The fat of the animal was burned and the hind quarter and breast went to feed the priests. The rest of the animal went to the worshipers in a sacred meal eaten on the Temple property. The blood of the animals was thrown against the base of the altar because it was a holy source of life. Various grains and vegetables were offered, with a small portion burned on the altar and the balance dedicated to the support of the priests. In some sacrifices wine was poured out at the base of the altar.

Contemporary Christians and Jews associate worship with words, dramatic movements and symbolic articles; the slaughter of animals, wood fires on the altar and more than small quantities of bread and wine jar our sensibilities. Though ancient Jewish sacrificial practice differed greatly from our customs, it fit perfectly into its world and age and reached to the very foundations of humanity and human life. Humans related to God in terms of life and death. Life came from God and returned to God. This primordial relationship found expression in sacred activities which involved blood, the death of animals, fire, and food. The special handling of consecrated animals and foods, the daily and yearly celebration of God's rule over humans and the deeply agricultural roots of Jewish worship symbolized life as primary to humans and totally dependent on God. A small example of this style of worship can be found in Luke 23:22–24 where Mary and Joseph go to the Temple forty days after Mary has given birth both to offer Jesus to God and to offer sacrifice (two small birds because they were poor) for ritual purification. "And when the time came for their purification according to the law of Moses, they brought him (Jesus) up to Jerusalem to present him to the Lord (as it is written in the law of the Lord, 'Every male that opens the womb shall be called holy to the Lord') and to offer a sacrifice according to what is said in the law of the Lord, 'a pair of turtledoves, or two young pigeons.' " The gift of a life required immediate and specific acknowledgment of the source of life, God.

Animal sacrifice has almost completely died out in recent centuries. We struggle to understand the meaning of slaughtering animals in honor of a god, much less the God of Judaism and Christianity. In antiquity people were more close to life and death than we are today. They killed their own animals for meat, personally buried their own dead and brought their own children into the world in their homes. They grew their own grain and fruit and knew the vagaries and dangers of life, death, growth and decay from first-hand experience. Naturally, they translated these experiences into symbolic acts which acknowledged the realities of their lives and their relationship to God. Bloody animal sacrifice, as well as the other offerings of grain, dough and wine, starkly recognizes that life itself and all that supports life come from God and are completely dependent on God. The relationship between God and humans relies on active recognition of human dependence and on a thankful reception of God's gifts. Though human offerings have come from God, nevertheless their return to God, and the very return of life itself to God, make an effective and lived statement difficult to duplicate in modern religious symbolism.

## Public Passover Celebration

On the day before Passover the Temple was extremely crowded with people and sacrificial animals. The usual afternoon prayers and sacrifices and the special festival prayers were conducted earlier than usual so that the sacrificing of Passover animals for the evening meal could begin at three o'clock. As they did every day, the priests offered a lamb which was completely burned on the altar. In addition they burned a cake of flour kneaded with oil and poured out some wine on the altar. These foods are the staples of the Palestinian diet and articulate the people's recognition that their lives are sustained by and dependent on God. Extra sacrifices were offered for the festival of Passover and the Levites accompanied all this activity with sung prayer. Jews pray standing up and most probably chanted hymns and psalms responsorially with the Levites. One group of psalms (120–134) are called the Songs of Ascents and were chanted by pilgrims. The third of these psalms summarizes their feelings:

I rejoiced because they said to me,
"We will go up to the house of the Lord."

And now we have set foot
    within your gates, O Jerusalem—
Jerusalem, built as a city
    with compact unity.

To it the tribes go up
    the tribes of the Lord,
According to the decree for Israel,
    to give thanks to the name of the Lord.
In it are set up judgment seats,
    seats for the house of David.

Pray for the peace of Jerusalem!
    May those who love you prosper!
May peace be within your walls,
    prosperity in your buildings.
Because of my relatives and friends
    I will say, "Peace be within you!"
Because of the house of the Lord, our God,
    I will pray for your good.

The rituals, the songs, the excitement of a journey to Jerusalem, the massive strength and sophisticated beauty of the architecture all made the festival spirit alive and palpable to the crowds.

At three o'clock the heads of each of the households which were to celebrate the Passover meal brought a lamb or kid to the Temple area. According to the highly systematized account in the later Jewish law code, the Mishna, because the Courtyard of the Israelites was small and the people so numerous, they had to be admitted in three groups. Another authority says that the animals were so many that the sacrificial period often had to be extended into dusk. The Passover sacrifice was unique among Jewish sacrifices because here only did private individuals perform the act of sacrifice. The priests tossed the blood of the animals at the base of the altar in the court above and offered the fat of the animal on the altar as they did with other sacrifices, but the heads of the household who brought the animals performed the ritual act of slaughter. The lamb (or sometimes goat) had to be a year old (interpreted by some to mean in its first year) and in perfect condition. No blemished or defective animal could be associated with the worship of God. The animals not only had to be killed but also flayed and butchered so that the prescribed parts could be offered and the rest of the meat prepared for the meal which followed during the evening.

The sacrificial activities in the Temple related intimately both to the family meal which was eaten subsequently and to the regular public worship in the Temple. The slaughter was accompanied by songs chanted by the Levites, such as this section from Psalm 118:

> I thank you that you have answered me
> > and have become my salvation.
> The stone which the builders rejected
> > has become the head of the corner.
> This is the Lord's doing;
> > it is marvelous in our eyes.
> This is the day which the Lord has made;
> > let us rejoice and be glad in it.
> Save us, we beseech you, O Lord!
> > O Lord, we beseech you, give us success.

The songs, the priests, the trumpets announcing the progress of the ritual, the crowds, the confusion, the smell, the heat, the dust and the noise from humans and animals are equally parts of life and the Temple ritual celebrating the God who gives life.

For Jews in Jesus' time the sacrifice of the Passover animal at the Temple and the eating of that animal during the evening meal were the center of the Passover celebration and symbolism. For the past nineteen centuries, since the Temple was destroyed, Jews have not had a Passover sacrifice as the center of the Passover celebration. We will explore how they made that adjustment in the next chapter. The emphasis on the sacrificed animal provided the early Christians with the motive and the imagery to understand Jesus' death as a Passover sacrifice to save humanity.

## The Passover Meal

Contemporary Jews cherish the Passover meal in the home as the most lively and emotionally laden celebration of their year. Its place in the memories and hearts of Jews may best be compared to Christmas among Christians. At the beginning of the meal ritual foods are displayed and consumed, prayers recited, instructions and explanations read and hymns sung. After the meal futher prayers and hymns extend the celebration until late in the evening. In the next chapter we shall read, understand and appreciate the parts of this ritual order (*Seder*) of Passover as it has been celebrated since the Temple was destroyed in 70 A.D. until the present.

In the time of Jesus, while the Temple still stood, the Passover meal with a sacrificial animal could only be eaten in Jerusalem after the animal was slaughtered and offered in the Temple. It is probable that many prayers and practices were common to the meal both before and after the loss of the Temple, but our direct knowledge of the Passover meal in Jesus' time is meager. A meal among believers following a sacrifice was quite normal in Judaism and other Near Eastern religions. Part of the animal was offered to the god as his portion and then the worshipers sat down in the house of the god (the temple) to share a meal with him. Similarly, Jews offered certain kinds of private sacrifices at the Temple during the year and they too ate the sacrificed animal on the Temple mount. These sacrificial meals allowed the participants to act out concretely and graphically their relationship with God. They actually ate in the holy place, the place where God's presence dwelt. They could communicate with God and enter into intimate communion with him. The society of God and humans in which humans receive from God and in a limited way enter into his divine life could be experienced and known both externally and internally. Personal communion was ratified by the community in its central place of worship. It is from this tradition of contact with God that the Christian Eucharistic meal grows.

The Samaritans, a group of sectarian Jews who originated before Jesus' birth, still sacrifice Passover lambs and eat the Passover meal. They believe that the proper place for sacrifice is Mount Gerezim in Samaria, north of Jerusalem, and not in the (now lost) Temple. A surviving group of several hundred still celebrate Passover on top of Mount Gerezim today. Clothed in white robes they gather on top of the mountain for the seven day Feast of Unleavened Bread which begins with the Passover sacrifice. Near dusk they pray and sing in praise of God. Their high priest, assisted by other priests, stands near a trench dug into the ground. The lambs for sacrifice are herded into the middle of the throng. A priest cuts the throat of the first lamb and holds up the bloody knife in the air as a signal that the sacrifices have begun. The people respond with a cheer and further song.

After the ceremony the animals are trussed up, their skins flayed off and their innards cleaned out and inspected for any irregularity which would render them ritually unfit. Then the animal carcasses are impaled on twelve foot wooden spits which are thrust upright into pits in the ground which contain fires. The pits are covered to form ovens and the animals are roasted for several hours. At midnight the participants put on heavy shoes, gird their loins (that is, put belts for traveling around their waists) and take staffs in their hands, as commanded by the Book of Exodus. They eat the roasted sacrificial animals, taking care not to break any bones, and burn the leftover meat and bones before dawn, all according to biblical rules. Though we do not know that their exact practices match those of the first century in Jerusalem, the journey to the top of the mountain, the ritual slaughter, the preparations and the adherence to biblical commands can give us some sense of what an ancient Passover was like.

In Jerusalem at Passover the crowds were so great that on that one evening the sacrificial meal could be eaten anywhere in Jerusalem, rather than just in the Temple. We are not sure how families outside of Jerusalem who had not made the pilgrimage for the festival celebrated Passover. One source from the second century B.C. suggests that the family part of the celebration had become much more important since pre-exilic times (the seventh century B.C.) and it may be that a meal without sacrificial victim was celebrated. However, we have no direct evidence for a Passover meal, similar to the later Seder, outside Jerusalem. We only know that Jews everywhere ate unleavened bread for seven days. We must use later sources to speculate about the exact kind of meal eaten for Passover while the Temple still stood and the Passover sacrifice was offered in Jerusalem.

The Bible directs that the group eating the meal be large enough to consume the animal. This meant ten to twenty people, most often an extended family of parents, children, and grandchildren. They gathered in rented rooms or sometimes in tents, anywhere a group could cook and eat a meal. The meal was eaten after dark because the Jewish day begins with sundown and extends until sundown the next day. Thus Passover begins in the evening. The group ate the foods prescribed in the Bible, the sacrificed animal, unleavened bread and bitter herbs. The unleavened bread was eaten both this evening and for the week following during the seven day festival of Unleavened Bread. The bitter herbs were eaten in small quantities as a reminder of slavery in Egypt. Since wine was the ordinary table drink in Palestine, we would assume that it was consumed as a matter of course. However, a second century B.C. document, the Book of Jubilees, mentions wine as important and necessary to the meal. The mention of wine, which is not part of the biblical ritual, indicates a shift in emphasis from public ritual to individual enjoyment and family celebration. The four required cups of wine which are central to the later Passover Seder derive from this early designation of wine as part of the ceremony.

We have later indications that some Passover customs had changed since early biblical times, but we are not sure which ones were followed in Jesus' time. The following account is probable. The Book of Exodus says that the Passover should be eaten with sandals and belt on, with staff in hand and in haste (12:11). This tense and unfestive style of meal recreated the haste of the last meal before the escape from Egypt. But the mood of the meal had changed over the centuries and taken on the atmosphere of a family celebration. The command to eat in haste was understood as a characteristic of the first Passover in Egypt only. In addition, the animal to be sacrificed and eaten was not set aside on the tenth of Nisan, four days earlier (Ex 12:4), nor, as far as we know, was blood from the animal smeared on the doorway. Finally, the Bible says that nothing from the Passover animal is to remain by morning, meaning that it must be completely eaten or the remains burned during the night. By the first century, respect for the Sabbath and festival days (as well as the large crowds) caused postponement of this duty until the day after the festival. The later rabbis recognized these changes and justified them by a distinction between the Passover in Egypt and Passover as it was observed in later generations (Mishnah Pesahim 9:5).

## The Order of the Meal

The Passover meal, like any festival meal, began with a blessing over wine, "Blessed are you, Lord our God, creator of the fruit of the vine." This was followed, or sometimes preceded, by a prayer praising God for the special day which was being celebrated, "With love you have given us, Lord our God . . . this day of the festival of unleavened bread, the season of our deliverance, a holy convocation in remembrance of the departure from Egypt." The exact texts of these prayers varied in the time of Jesus; the selections given here come from the Passover Seder used by Jews today. This Seder, which is a descendant of the Passover ritual used by Jesus and his contemporaries, will be presented and explained in the next chapter. Here we will look briefly at some of the early parts of the Passover ritual most probably recited by Jesus and his friends.

We do not know the order of events in the Passover meal during the first century. Even the Gospel accounts of Jesus last meal which imply that it was a Passover meal fail to give a complete account of what went on. The Seder, or order of the meal, used by Jews today puts a large body of instruction and prayer before the meal. There is some evidence that all of this was done after the meal in Jesus' time. The contemporary Seder has four cups of wine consumed at intervals during the ritual and meal. We know that wine was served but we are not sure that four cups was the practice in the first century.

Since it was a festive meal, the Passover probably began with hors d'oeuvres which consisted of a vegetable such as lettuce dipped in vinegar or some kind of sauce. This may have been served with an initial cup of wine. The meal followed, initiated by a blessing said over the bread, "Blessed are you, Lord our God, who brings forth bread from the earth." The participants in the meal fulfilled the biblical commandments for Passover by eating the animal which had been sacrificed, unleavened bread and bitter herbs. The meal proper concluded with a blessing over a cup of wine. If Jesus' Last Supper with his disciples was a Passover meal, it is likely that these two blessings, the grace before the meal over the bread and the grace after the meal over the cup of wine, were the occasion for his declaration that bread and wine are his body and blood. The eating and drinking of them became a memorial act, just as the Passover itself is a memorial.

After the meal, its meaning was explained and the story of the first Passover told. The Seder and other early rabbinic documents contain several explanations which were used at the discretion of the leader of each Seder and expounded in his own words. Instruction concerning Passover is mandated by the Bible which says that the meaning of the unleavened bread and of the Passover sacrifice must be explained. Concerning the unleavened bread, "You shall tell your son on that day, 'It is because of what the Lord did for me when I came out of Egypt' " (Ex 13:8). Similarly, the Passover sacrifice is to be explained, "When your children say to you, 'What do you mean by this service?' you shall say, 'It is the sacrifice of the Lord's Passover, for he passed over the houses of the people of Israel in Egypt when he slew the Egyptians but spared our houses' " (Ex 12:26–27). A meal with its symbolic acts gives substance to the festival in honor of God's saving of Israel in Egypt.

The instruction was probably initiated by three questions. Someone at the meal asked why the Passover animal was roasted rather than boiled, why the bread was unleavened and why vegetables were dipped and eaten during the meal as well as before the meal when they served as hors d'oeuvres. Contrary to modern tastes, boiled meat was preferred to roasted, probably because tough range animals were thus tenderized. But the people in Egypt were in a rush to leave, so they hurriedly roasted the animals. Likewise, the rush to leave Egypt did not allow enough time for them to put yeast in their bread and wait for it to rise. The second serving of vegetable and herbs is the ritual consumption of the bitter herbs. These three extraordinary practices are commanded by Exodus 12:8, "They shall eat the flesh that night, roasted; with unleavened bread and bitter herbs they shall eat it," and the three questions highlight them.

In Jesus' time the answers to the questions were probably not set formulae. The most general instruction is that the explanation is to begin with ignominy and end with glory. Two traditional replies to the questions which are preserved in the Passover Seder fulfill that requirement though neither answers the questions directly. One recounts the saving of Israel in Egypt.

We were Pharaoh's slaves in Egypt, and the Lord our God brought us forth from there with a mighty hand and outstretched arm. And if the Holy One, blessed be He, had not brought our forefathers forth from Egypt, then we, our children and our children's children would still be Pharaoh's slaves in Egypt.

Israel began in slavery (ignominy) and ended up free and in possession of their own land (glory).

The other explanation looks to God's original call to Abraham to leave the worship of other gods (ignominy) and serve only Yahweh God (glory). "In the beginning our fathers were idolators, but now the Omnipresent has drawn us to his service." This primordial relationship underlies all else in Israel's history and marks the radical change which ultimately brings Israel into existence. Not only the events in Egypt, but the very identity and character of the Jewish people is preserved in and symbolized by the Passover celebration. Celebration of Passover is an affirmation of God's very existence.

A description of four types of sons and what they ask their fathers concerning the festival symbolizes a variety of responses to the Passover ritual. The four sons are wise, wicked, simple and not able to ask. All four, and most prominently the wise and wicked, appear in the wisdom literature such as the Book of Proverbs and Sirach. The contrast of types, such as the wise and foolish, occurs in the New Testament, later Jewish literature and Greco-Roman literature. The descriptions of the four sons indirectly instruct the participants in the correct response to the Passover story.

The wise son wishes to know the rules for Passover and their meaning, something the tradition wishes each Jew to master. The wicked son asks an implicitly hostile question, "What is this service *to you?*" By excluding himself from the group celebrating he also denies the relevance of the festival for himself and so denies God's relationship to himself and implicitly God's existence. The ritual says that if he had been in Egypt, he would not have been redeemed. The simple child just asks "What is this?" and the head of the household responds with the story of the Exodus. With a child who does not know enough to ask, you begin the Exodus story yourself. The characters described are stereotypes but the responses to be given them are not; the events of the Exodus from Egypt and their meaning for Israel must live on in each participant. As the ritual says later, "In every generation each person must look to himself/herself as if he/she came forth out of Egypt." Without this attitude the Passover will die.

The original Passover experience, escape from destruction at the hands of the Egyptians, is widened and deepened by an extended midrash on Deuteronomy 26:5–8. A midrash is an interpretation of a biblical passage, line by line and often phrase by phrase, in order to bring out subtle meanings in the text and more importantly apply the text to a new situation in which the listeners find themselves. Deuteronomy 26:5–8 is a description of their ancestors used by Israelites when they brought certain offerings to the Temple. The passage speaks first of Abraham, Isaac and Jacob, the patriarchs and earliest ancestors of the Israelites. They were from an ethnic group called Arameans who were found in northern Syria and Iraq.

> A wandering Aramean was my father; and he went down into Egypt and sojourned there, few in number; and there he became a nation, great, mighty, and populous. And the Egyptians treated us harshly, and afflicted us, and laid upon us hard bondage. Then we cried to the Lord the God of our fathers, and the Lord heard our voice, and saw our affliction, our toil, and our oppression; and the Lord brought us out of Egypt with a mighty hand and an outstretched arm, with great terror, with signs and wonders.

The self-description goes on to acknowledge that God gave the Israelites a fertile land, Israel, and so they in turn bring God the first fruits from their land to acknowledge God's gift.

Before hearing a detailed interpretation of this passage the participants in the meal raise their cups and affirm their faith in God's care, "It is this promise (to free Israel from Egypt) which has stood by our fathers and by us. For it was not one man only (that is, Pharaoh) who stood up against us to destroy us; in every generation they stand up against us to destroy us, and the Holy One, blessed be He, (that is, God) saves us from their hand." Each participant must identify with the Exodus salvation because each person needs this same kind of salvation in each generation.

To prove the continuing need for salvation, the first phrase, "A wandering Aramean was my father," receives a striking interpretation. In Genesis Abraham, Isaac and Jacob are not explicitly identified as Arameans but Jacob's uncle Laban is. Laban is an ambiguous character because he cheats Jacob (and Jacob successfully cheats him in return). The midrash turns him into a villain and enemy of Israel. The Hebrew word for "wandering" can easily be read (with a change of vowels) as "would have destroyed" thus yielding the sense "An Aramean (Laban) would have destroyed my father (Jacob)." Laban joins Pharaoh on the list of those who have persecuted and sought to destroy Judaism. This interpretation encourages the listeners to add other names to the list from their own generation, for in every age Jews need salvation from hostile forces. Thus the Passover experience repeats itself in each of the participants every time the ritual is reenacted.

The redemption from Egypt is celebrated by the singing of the Hallel. The Hallel ("Praise") is a sequence of psalms (113–118) which praise God for saving Israel and for his constant care. In it the believers express their confidence in God and acknowledge him as their God and Savior. The Hallel was sung by the Levites in the Temple during the afternoon Passover sacrifices and later, perhaps during the first century, became part of the private meals which followed the public sacrifices. Psalm 114 contains an explicit mention of the deliverance from Pharaoh in Egypt and exemplifies the spirit of the whole:

When Israel went forth from Egypt,
the house of Jacob from a people of strange language,
Judah became his sanctuary,
Israel his dominion.

The sea looked and fled,
Jordan turned back.
The mountains skipped like rams,
the hills like lambs.

What ails you, O sea, that you flee?
O Jordan, that you turn back?
O mountains, that you skip like rams?
O hills, like lambs?

After the singing of the Hallel, the festivities may have been concluded by a final cup of wine (the fourth cup in the present Passover Seder). Custom now and most probably then dictated that this was to be the last cup of wine.

Other regulations forbid going to other houses to drink and party. The normal custom on a holiday or at a celebration was to stay up most of the night drinking and to join with other groups reveling. This practice is called *afikomen*. In the modern Seder *afikomen* has become the desert of matzah. In order to keep the spirit of the day holy this normal practice is forbidden. In his last meal with his disciples Jesus uses this prohibition of revelry to make a larger point when he says, "I shall not drink again of the fruit of the vine until that day when I drink it anew in the Kingdom of God" (Mk 14:25). The Passover is the last celebration of Jesus and his disciples within Judaism according to the New Testament writers because the sacrifice of Jesus will inaugurate the Kingdom of God and a new order. Mark narrates the end of the meal simply: "When they had sung a hymn, they went out to the Mount of Olives" (Mk 14:26). The hymn was the Hallel; when Jesus and his disciples had finished the meal in their rented room, they did not drink into the night or join other groups, but left their borrowed room and went off to pray on the Mount of Olives right next to the city of Jerusalem.

The Passover celebrated by Jesus and his disciples reaches back to sacrifices and celebration observed by long lost people who lived before Abraham and Moses. The interpretation given to the Passover by the early Christians reaches forward to the second coming of Jesus and the completion of God's Kingdom. For Jews in Jesus' time and for him and his disciples the Passover meal reinforced and celebrated their identity as Jews, descended from Abraham, saved by God in Egypt, led by God through his revelation to Moses on Sinai, given a land and a way of life, instructed, protected, punished, forgiven and cherished through centuries, free because of God's love even while subjugated within the Roman Empire.

The Passover included sacrifice, blood, bread, all the realities of life (and death). This very Jewish sacred time and ritual was taken by a Jew sent by God and transformed by him and his followers into a new feast with analogous meaning. The Easter of the Lord's resurrection celebrates his sacrifice and is commemorated by his meal with his friends. By it God's Christian people are saved as God's Jewish people were saved before. Without the rich milieu of grain and herd, prayer and sacrifice, wine and family Jesus could not have communicated his message and mission nor could his early followers have understood him. Jesus celebrated the Passover and the writers of the New Testament understood him as the Passover lamb.

# 4

# *The Passover Seder*

Jews today celebrate the same Passover celebrated by Jesus. The manner of celebration has undergone a long evolution. After a brief sketch of some major adaptations in the tradition we shall examine the major sections of the contemporary Passover Seder in order to understand its spirit and meaning. The Seder keeps alive the memory and reality of the first Passover just as Easter brings close Jesus' own Passover sacrifice.

The word *Seder* means "order" in Hebrew. The Passover Seder is the order of prayers and events which make up the Passover meal. The Passover Seders we have now represent several traditions which have varied greatly over the centuries. Favorite songs of certain communities were added to the Seder. Additional explanations of the ritual and history were appended to important passages. Local customs, prayers and blessings influenced how the participants expressed themselves, and changing theological emphases and needs led to reformulations of many passages. Some of the central prayers, actions and interpretations probably date from the time of Jesus (see the previous chapter), though certainty eludes us.

The major shift in the way of celebrating Passover occurred when the Temple was destroyed in 70 A.D. because the Passover lamb could no longer be sacrificed at the Temple. That meant that the main course of the meal and the symbolic center of the worship was lost. The earliest certain record we have of adaptation to this traumatic loss is the Mishna, the collection of Jewish law from about 200 A.D.

The Mishna simply assumes an answer to the major question facing Judaism and in assuming the answer emphatically argues for it: the celebration of Passover should continue even without the Passover sacrifice which formed the center of the meal. It may seem obvious to us centuries later that Passover would continue, but all the other Temple sacrifices and meals ceased and were commemorated as synagogue services. The same could be expected for the Passover meal which was no longer needed because the Temple and Jerusalem where it was eaten were no more.

The Mishna which allows celebration of the Passover meal outside Jerusalem without the Passover lamb makes major changes in the tradition. But the rules for Passover are articulated in the Mishna as though there were no change from biblical times. Rules for celebrating Passover in the Temple and later rules for the family celebration of Passover are intertwined. Subtle adjustments are made to allow for the absence of the sacrificed animal. The time of the meal is kept the same as that celebrated in Jerusalem. The unleavened bread and bitter herbs are treated as of equal value and importance with the Passover lamb. Since both are available, the absence of the lamb ceases to be critical. The questions concerning the celebration asked by the child are revised to fit the new order of worship. Wine increases in importance as a source of joy and symbolic value (as does the unleavened bread), and the psalms which were sung at the sacrifice in the Temple are now sung during the meal by the participants. As much as possible of the Temple ritual is transferred to the home and the rest is replaced with new elements.

Rabbinic Judaism, the style of Judaism which developed through the Mishna and eventually dominated the whole Jewish tradition until the last century, added its own tone to the ceremonies. Rabbinic Judaism placed study of Scripture and law at the center of its way of life and worship. Consequently, the Passover Seder contains added sections which instruct the participants on just how the ceremony is to be done and the reasons for doing so. Midrashic interpretations of Scripture are added at certain points and the core of the early ceremony becomes the interpretation of Deuteronomy 26 on how God saved Israel. So important is this biblical exegesis that the Passover Seder is often called the Passover Haggada. A haggada is an interpretation of a non-legal section of Scripture. Blessings were added at each juncture of the ceremony, in accordance with the rabbinic stress on the blessing as a preeminent mode of prayer. Finally, the theme of redemption, based on the redemption of Israel from Egypt, undergoes a reorientation so that the major stress is on future redemption, both the redemption of Israel in exile and the final eschatological redemption when God brings justice in his Kingdom. Perhaps this emphasis on the future explains the curious omission of Moses in the Exodus story. It is God who redeemed in the past and who will redeem in the future.

As a response to the disruption of society caused by the destruction of Jerusalem and the Temple in 70 A.D. the Passover Seder unifies society and levels distinctions by inviting all to the table as equals and by asserting that all need redemption equally. The normal social distinctions and oppressive experiences are left behind as the believers go on pilgrimage into the Passover festival. The Mishna and the Passover Seder both respond to the dangers of social dissolution and disorder by moving into a timeless, cultic world where reality has not changed and where the ceremonies of Passover are treated as if they had always been this way.

## *The Contemporary Passover Seder*

For the Christian reader the Passover Seder provides several parallels to Christian worship. Salvation and redemption are central interests and bread is a major symbol. Scripture is read, remembered and relived in the participation of the community. Prayer and ritual action point to God's mercy in the past and to the hope of his care in the future. Some of the elements of the Seder have already been presented in the previous chapter and will be more briefly explained here.

The Seder begins with a blessing, as does any meal. In this case the wine, so central to the celebration, is blessed with special reference to the Exodus which is being remembered.

> Blessed are you, Lord our God, king of the universe. . . . With love you have given us, Lord our God, holidays for gladness, festivals and seasons for rejoicing, this day of the festival of unleavened bread, the season of deliverance, a holy convocation in remembrance of the departure from Egypt.

The cup of wine which is drunk after this blessing is the first of four which will mark major transitions in the course of the evening.

After the first cup of wine the participants prepare for the meal by a ritual washing of their hands. Then they eat some raw vegetables as an hors d'oeuvre. This was a common custom in antiquity. After the hors d'oeuvres, attention immediately turns to the unleavened bread. After the Temple and Passover lamb were lost, the unleavened bread came more and more to replace the Passover lamb symbolically. The master of the Seder breaks the middle one of the three large wafers of unleavened bread on the platter in front of him and sets it aside for *afikomen,* which is now interpreted as dessert. Then the platter of bread is held up, along with a shankbone and an egg, and all are invited to join in the meal.

> This is the bread of poverty (or affliction) which our forefathers ate in the land of Egypt. Let all who are hungry enter and eat; let all who are needy come to our Passover feast. This year we are here; next year may we be in the Land of Israel. This year we are slaves; next year may we be free men.

The unleavened bread bears a symbolic weight which it did not have when the Temple was still standing and participants sat with the Passover lamb roasted on the table. Now salvation and redemption from oppression are not symbolized concretely by the lamb, but by the bread which the master of the Seder holds up. The unleavened bread (matzah) has become a symbol for salvation and for God's presence, past and future, among his people. This theme continues through the Seder. The invitation to eat bread functions in another way. When the lamb was sacrificed at the Temple, all those who were to eat of the lamb had to be present and constitute themselves a Passover group. Now the invitation to partake of the matzah replaces that gathering at the Temple.

The presence of unusual foodstuff on the table and special ritual activities prompt a ritual set of questions from the youngest member of the company celebrating Passover. "Why does this night differ from all other nights?" In earlier times three questions were probably asked. But since the ceremony has been modified, so are the questions. Four things need explanation:

On all other nights we eat either leavened or unleavened bread;
    why on this night only unleavened bread?
On all other nights we eat all kinds of herbs;
    why on this night only bitter herbs?
On all other nights we need not dip our herbs even once;
    why on this night must we dip them twice?
On all other nights we eat either sitting up or reclining;
    why on this night do we all recline?

The last question manifests a change from the biblical custom which required the participants to eat standing, ready for travel. By this point Jews are following the Greco-Roman custom of reclining on couches at festive meals. Ordinarily, herbs (vegetables) were offered to the guest as an hors d'oeuvre; as that custom fell into disuse, the child asked both about the first course and also about the bitter herbs eaten later in the ceremony as a symbol of the oppression in Egypt. The first two questions refer to the main symbolic elements of the meal, unleavened bread and *bitter* herbs.

The master of the Seder gives two answers to the questions: the story of the redemption of Israel from Egypt and the story of how God called Abraham to worship him instead of idols. After the first explanation, the Exodus story, the Seder has two stories of rabbis discussing the meaning of the Seder. Since study of the Torah, the Bible and its related traditions, is a central act of piety and worship for the rabbis, the presence of these two stories bespeaks their interest in Passover. Passover must be understood accurately as well as celebrated, so the middle of the celebration is a most appropriate place to clarify disputes and add insights. The Seder, which has replaced the Passover sacrifice in the Temple, must itself be carefully guarded by informed participants.

The description of the four sons, each of whom has a different attitude toward the Seder, further emphasizes the need for active participation in the Passover ritual for it to be effective. Simple remembering or rote actions are insufficient. The child too young to ask must be told the Exodus story. The child too simple to remember or understand must be reminded of God's redemption of Israel in Egypt. The child who does not identify with the participants is not one of them and is not redeemed. The wise child asks about the laws of Passover and is instructed in exactly how and why to proceed. That is, the wise child can fully and truly carry on Passover. This type of person knows the past history and present ritual and the future meaning of Passover for all Israel united in celebration. Knowledge and faith meet in ritual action on Passover evening.

Instruction of the participants in the Passover Seder continues with a long interpretation of Deuteronomy 26:5–8, a passage which tells the story of Israel's slavery in Egypt and God's redemption of them. The midrash or haggada on Deuteronomy 26 has given the Passover Seder its alternate name, the Passover Haggada. Each phrase and even word of this brief scriptural passage is related to the salvation from Egypt and also to Jacob's conflicts with Laban (Gen 28—31). The summary of the Exodus story contained in Deuteronomy is expanded with quotations from the Book of Exodus so that the complete story is told with great stress on Israel's need and God's power. The detailed account of what God did for Israel is amplified and emphasized by a list of the ten plagues which God brought on the Egyptians, and the whole recital is climaxed by a playful and joyful hymn of fourteen stanzas. Each stanza enumerates something God did and ends with the refrain that this one thing would have been enough. But God did more. The rising crescendo of God's generous activity for Israel ends with a review of all God has done and a repetition of Israel's debt of thanks.

> How many are the claims of the Omnipresent upon our thankfulness!
> Had He taken us out of Egypt,
>     but not executed judgments on them,
>         We should have been content!
> Had He executed judgments on them,
>     but not on their gods,
>         We should have been content!
> Had He executed judgments on their gods,
>     but not slain their first-born,
>         We should have been content!

Had He slain their first-born,
>but not given us their substance,
>>We should have been content!
Had He given us their substance,
>but not torn the Sea apart for us,
>>We should have been content!

The hymn ends breathlessly with a paragraph repeating each of the fifteen items contained in the fourteen stanzas. The participants end by laughing at their own attempts to race through the repetition of the whole song in one long rush:

Then how much more, doubled and redoubled, is the claim the Omnipresent has upon our thankfulness! For he did take us out of Egypt, and execute judgments on them, and judgments on their gods, and slay their first-born, and give us their substance, and tear the Sea apart for us, and bring us through it dry, and sink our oppressors in the midst of it, and satisfy our needs in the desert for forty years, and feed us manna, and give us the Sabbath, and bring us to Mount Sinai, and give us the Torah, and bring us into the Land of Israel, and build us the House of his choosing to atone for all our sins.

The recital of the past, of the original Passover and redemption from Egypt, has been repeated in several ways, as a simple summary of the story, as an elaborate scriptural interpretation and as a joyful and humorous hymn. Now the celebrants return to the present and the symbols on the table.

Once more the fundamental instructions for celebrating Passover are repeated. Rabban Gamaliel, a prominent teacher of the late first and early second century, summarized the requirements for Passover after the Temple had been destroyed: "Whoever does not make mention of the following three things on Passover has not fulfilled his obligation: namely, the Passover sacrifice, unleavened bread and bitter herbs." Note that unleavened bread and bitter herbs are given equal importance with the Passover sacrifice. Since the Passover sacrifice can no longer be offered, it must be supplemented and supported by other symbols which are present on the table. The master of the Seder puts Gamaliel's instructions into practice first by speaking of the Passover sacrifice which used to be offered when the Temple stood. Then he holds up the unleavened bread and explains the reason for it in terms of the redemption in Egypt:

> The dough of our fathers had not yet leavened when the King over all kings, the Holy One, blessed be He, revealed himself to them and redeemed them.

Finally, he holds up the bitter herbs and teaches that they symbolize the oppression suffered in Egypt. Christians will note ritual similarities with the liturgy in which bread and wine are raised up and presented to the congregation as sacramental symbols of Jesus' sacrifice and presence to the participants. In both contexts the symbols gain their meaning from intimate participation.

> In every generation let each person look on himself as if he came forth from Egypt, as it is said: "And you shall tell your son in that day, saying: 'It is because of that which the Lord did for *me* when I came forth out of Egypt'" (Ex 13:8). It was not only our father that the Holy One, blessed be He, redeemed, but us as well did he redeem along with them, as it is said: "And he brought *us* out from thence, that He might bring us in, to give us the land which He swore unto our fathers" (Dt 6:23).

Now identified with the Israelites who escaped from Egypt, the participants in the Passover praise God and sing the first two psalms of the Hallel, a series of psalms (113–118) which praise God for his benevolent activities.

> Therefore, we are bound to thank, praise, laud, glorify, exalt, honor, bless, extol, and adore Him who performed all these miracles for our fathers and for us. He has brought us forth from slavery to freedom, from sorrow to joy, from mourning to holiday, from darkness to great light, and from bondage to redemption. Let us then recite before him a new song: Hallelujah.

After chanting the two psalms (113–114) which had originally been sung by the Levites in the Temple during the Passover sacrifice, the participants again express confidence in God's power to redeem them, but this time in the future.

> Blessed are you, O Lord, our God, king of the universe, who redeemed us and who redeemed our fathers from Egypt, and has brought us to this night, to eat thereon unleavened bread and bitter herbs. So, O Lord our God and God of our fathers, bring us to other festivals and holy days that come toward us in peace, happy in the building of your city and joyous in your service. And there may we eat of the sacrifices and paschal offerings, whose blood will come unto the wall of your altar for acceptance. Then shall we give thanks to you with a new song, for our redemption and the liberation of our soul.

The participants look back to how the Passover was celebrated in Jerusalem and forward to coming feasts in the hope that they will again worship God properly. Implicit in this prayer is the hope that Israel will be freed from the political forces which have destroyed the Temple and keep them from independence and security. The oppression suffered in Egypt has been repeated many times and requires constant redemption from God.

The participants end their praise of God with a cup of wine, the sign of joy, and then turn to the Passover meal itself. First the unleavened bread and then the bitter herbs are presented and eaten. After this both are eaten again in a sandwich, according to Hillel's way of obeying Numbers 9:11, "They shall eat it (the Passover sacrifice) with unleavened bread and bitter herbs." In fact, the second piece of matzah (unleavened bread) which makes the sandwich may symbolize the Passover sacrifice. After the ritual foods are consumed, the rest of the meal is eaten.

The meal concludes, as do all meals, with the grace or blessing of God: "Blessed are you, O Lord our God, king of the world, who feeds the entire world in his goodness, with grace, loving-kindness, and compassion. He gives bread to all flesh, for his mercy is forever." The blessings continue at length, thanking God first for food, then for the redemption from Egypt and finally asking God's pity on Israel for their present losses: "Take pity, O

Lord our God, on Israel, your people, and on Jerusalem, your city, and on Zion, the habitation of your glory, and on the kingdom of the House of David, your anointed, and upon the great and holy House over which your name is called." This blessing and subsequent ones pray that God will rescue and restore Jerusalem, the Messiah and the people of Israel. The bread and sacrifice of Passover symbolize future salvation as well as the past in a way similar to the bread and wine of Christian worship. After the grace, the third cup of wine is drunk and then the last four psalms of the Hallel (115–118) are sung, along with other songs. At the end of the ceremonies a fourth cup of wine is drunk and the participants express their yearning for salvation in the last petition, "Next year in Jerusalem."

The Passover Seder combines and integrates many aspects of Jewish belief and practice. Past and future rise up in the present. The words and actions represent what happened at the first Passover and what Jews have done yearly since. The participants are there at the first Passover and are personally saved by God; equally God saves them now from slavery, oppression or threat. All trust and hope that God will save them finally and perfectly in the future. The unleavened bread and bitter herbs express Israel's danger and suffering in Egypt as well as its eschatological hope for salvation. In all of the prayers and rituals of Passover God plays the central role. God saved the people of Israel in the past, cares for them now and will finally redeem them in the end.

# 5

# *Passover in the Gospels*

Christians especially value the Jewish Passover festival because Jesus died and rose during Passover. The Christian belief that Jesus' death atoned for humanity's sins and that his resurrection has given us new life grows out of Jewish belief. In the first Passover, God saved the Hebrew people. The Passover ritual associates this original act of salvation with all the subsequent times God saved Israel. Jesus' death during the Passover season has linked the two traditions inextricably. Early Christian writers in the New Testament set the narrative of Jesus' death and resurrection within the Passover festival and more importantly adapted the earlier biblical imagery and meaning to Jesus. The death of a human being means little in itself and a resurrection is incomprehensible without some explanation and a context to give it meaning. The explanation of what really happened when Jesus died and rose and how it affected us drew upon biblical sacrificial practices, especially the sacrificial meals held in the Temple and the Passover celebration. Jews worshiped and understood God through traditional practices which formed the foundation for the similar Christian understanding of God's love and activity.

Jesus certainly died and rose around the time of Passover, but the New Testament does not clearly tell us whether Jesus' last meal with his followers was a Passover meal or not. Even if it was not, the early Christian believers and the later Gospel writers who recorded their traditions and beliefs linked the final hours of Jesus with the Passover celebration and used Passover symbolism and allusions to understand Jesus' actions. This is natural because the earliest Christians were actually Jews who believed that Jesus was the Messiah, that is, the anointed one, appointed by God and sent to save God's people from evil by bringing about a time of justice and peace. These early believers, who included the Twelve and the other disciples mentioned in the Gospels and Acts of the Apostles, were not yet a socially distinct group which could be named Christian. They were a sub-group or sect of Judaism, following the teachings of their leader and believing in the extraordinary claims and deeds of Jesus who had himself been a Jew. They are called followers of a new "way" (Acts 9:2) and also "believers" (Acts 5:14), but they do not have a proper name because they are not yet a distinct religion or religious tradition which can be separated from Judaism. Only later, in Antioch (a non-Jewish city), did the followers of Jesus, many of whom were Gentiles, receive the nickname "Christians" (Acts 11:26). The early followers of Jesus in Jerusalem continued attending the Temple and were under the authority of the Jewish religious authorities who tried to suppress them. Even Paul, who preached to non-Jews in Asia Minor and Greece, customarily went to the synagogue in each town and to the Temple when he visited Jerusalem (Acts 13:14; 21:23–26).

A generation or two after Jesus when the Gospels were written (the 80's and 90's A.D.) Christians without a Jewish background still were familiar with Jewish traditions, including Passover, and expressed themselves in Jewish terms. The Bible, which was read at Christian worship, was what we now call the Old Testament. This was and is the word of God, the revelation in which God formed his people, Israel. According to *Christian* interpretation, the Bible foretold the coming of a Savior, Jesus. The first Christian generations did not have the collection of documents we now call the New Testament because these documents were still being written and so had not yet been gathered together and recognized as authoritative by the scattered Christian communities. Since Jesus and his first followers were Jews, the traditions about Jesus, which were eventually gathered and ordered into four Gospels, were set in a Jewish milieu and expressed through Jewish metaphors, ideas and practices. Any non-Jew who believed in Jesus became familiar with Jewish tradition. The same is true today for any Christian who celebrates a weekly day of worship, hears the Bible read in a church and prays to the God who saves his people. The weekly day of worship, the reading of the Bible in public and the belief in one God derive from Judaism and still link the two religious communities together in a broad common tradition. These links endure despite some Christians who tried to break the link with Judaism.

## The Gospel Traditions

The four Gospels contain a variety of teachings and stories about Jesus. This can be seen in the Gospel of John which differs greatly in its contents and literary modes of expression from the other three Gospels. The Gospels of Mark, Matthew and Luke are often referred to as the Synoptic Gospels because they have much in common, a fact which can be observed at a glance when they are set in parallel columns. The references to the Passover in the Synoptic Gospels are found mostly in the story of Jesus' death and the events surrounding it. Mark and Matthew are very similar to one another. Luke has a number of separate traditions and John even more. We shall look at each Gospel in turn, beginning with Mark, because Mark is the earliest Gospel (about 70 A.D.) and was used as a source by both Matthew and Luke. Just because Mark was composed as a whole document before any of the others does not mean that his traditions are the earliest, however. All the Gospel writers drew on forty or fifty years of teachings about Jesus which were passed on orally and in writings now lost. These teachings and stories underwent gradual modification to fit new needs and new questions and their verbal expression changed with author and style. Thus both Luke and John may have some interpretations of Jesus' death and resurrection which are earlier than those in Mark.

## The Gospel of Mark

Though Mark tells the story of Jesus in a matter of fact way, he does not just tack on the death of Jesus at the end of his story (chapters 14–15). He prepares us to understand the larger meaning of Jesus' death in the previous chapter in which Jesus talks about the end of the world and the condemna-

ah. Thus, Jesus entered Jerusalem as one coming in God's name, as one helping to reestablish David's kingdom and as one who is anointed. The anointing is ambiguous because it is both for Jesus' death and for his appointment as Messiah. This ambiguity corresponds to one of Mark's major themes, that Jesus is a *suffering* Messiah who will die and rise.

The day the Passover lambs were to be sacrificed in Jerusalem, Jesus sent his disciples to arrange for a room in which to celebrate the Passover meal. Jesus and his disciples were indistinguishable from thousands of other pilgrims who had to find a room somewhere in Jerusalem in which to eat the ritual Passover meal. The disciples were to approach a householder and ask to use the guest room which was "a large upper room furnished and ready," and then to prepare the meal.

### A Passover Meal?

Though Mark pictures Jesus' final meal with his disciples as a Passover meal, we are not certain that the final supper was a Passover. Jesus celebrates the Passover meal with his disciples in the evening because the Passover feast began at sundown and ran until the sundown of the next day. The next day, on Passover he was crucified. Matthew and Luke follow Mark's chronology. The Gospel of John says, on the contrary, that the day on which Jesus was crucified was the preparation day on which the Passover lamb was sacrificed (Jn 19:14; see also 18:28). Thus, Jesus' meal with his disciples would not have been a Passover meal, but an ordinary meal the evening before the Passover meal. Both John and the Synoptic Gospels have other statements which are hard to interpret. John says both that it was the preparation day for the Sabbath (19:31) and that it was the preparation day (19:42). Mark 15:42 and Luke 23:54 note that Joseph of Arimathea hurried Jesus' burial because it was the preparation day for the Sabbath. Matthew 27:62 says more cryptically that the next day was the day after the preparation day, but he does not say preparation for what. Sabbath ordinarly means the weekly Jewish day of worship from sundown Friday until sundown Saturday. The term Sabbath can also refer to any other feasts solemn enough to forbid work. The feast of Passover/Unleavened Bread is one of these "Sabbath feasts." All the sources have a tradition that the day on which Jesus died was a preparation day for a Jewish feast, but whether it was the Passover itself or a Sabbath which fell during Passover is uncertain. The Synoptic Gospels treat the meal as a Passover meal, but John places the meal a day earlier.

It seems likely that John is correct, though the conflict in the Gospel traditions must leave us uncertain. The evening during which the Passover was eaten and the day following were a most solemn festival. That the high priest and prominent Jewish leaders would have sent out troops to arrest Jesus, held private hearings and consultations, run an early morning court session and then entered into negotiations with Pilate is highly unlikely. John's tradition, that the day on which Jesus' died was the preparation day for the Passover and that the next day was a Sabbath in the sense that it was a solemn feast (Passover), is more probable. In keeping with this view John does not suggest that the meal is a Passover meal nor does he recount Jesus' blessings over the bread and wine. Rather he shows Jesus preparing his disciples for his death by washing their feet and instructing them at length.

Why did Mark's tradition about Jesus, which he passed on to Matthew and Luke, conceive of Jesus' last meal with his disciples as a Passover meal? After Jesus' death and resurrection Jesus' followers remembered the last meal with Jesus as symbolic of his death and resurrection and they gathered together regularly to eat as they had with Jesus, to remember what Jesus had done and to instruct themselves in its meaning. Since Jesus had died at Passover, like the Passover lamb, and since Jesus' death saved them from sin as the Passover lamb saved them from the angel of death in Egypt (Ex 12:1–13), the early Christians used the story and symbols of Exodus and Passover to explain what Jesus had done for his followers. As Moses had led the people of Israel to safety and instructed them in God's word, so Jesus did the same. Freedom from Egypt and salvation from Pharaoh's armies became freedom from sin and salvation from punishment for sin. Passover and the Passover lamb became the Eucharist and Jesus. Not all of this theology is explicit in Mark and some of it is only later developed in detail. However, the transformation of the Jewish Passover into the Christian Easter began with the identification of Jesus' last meal with the Passover meal. Even if this identification is not historically true, it is theologically true.

*Jesus' Meal with the Twelve*

Though a meal symbolizes unity, friendship and life, Jesus' meal with his twelve disciples cannot be separated from the painful events about to transpire. Jesus predicts that he will be betrayed and acknowledges that this is necessary and has meaning. "The Son of man goes as it is written of him." Son of man is a title for the heavenly figure who will be sent by God in the end to rule over the kingdom (see Dn 7). Mark spent much of his Gospel showing that the Son of man, Jesus, must suffer and die (i.e., go) before God's Kingdom can fully come (see especially 8:27—10:52). Even at an intimate and final moment with his disciples, Jesus never forgets nor can he separate himself from the larger and cosmic dimension to his life and activity. To eat the Lord's supper means to remember the death of Jesus with all its effects for us.

The account of Jesus' meal with his disciples is not detailed or complete (Mk. 14:1–31). Jesus' most memorable and important actions are narrated in order to prepare us for his death and instruct the reader in its meaning. If the supper was a Passover meal, we have no full account of the Passover ritual used, nor of the course of the meal. The only description of their meal is Jesus' ritual feeding of his disciples. The symbolic statements, "This is my body. . . . This is my blood," almost certainly derive from the liturgical formulae used by early Christians in their worship after Jesus' death. The words of Jesus in Mark and Matthew are very similar to each other. Those found in Luke and Paul form another tradition which differs slightly from that in Mark and Matthew. Both traditions contain early and concise explanations of the meaning of what Jesus did, both at the supper and in his death.

*The Sacrifice*

If with Mark we understand Jesus' last supper as a Passover meal, then after the initial Passover ritual (the Seder), Jesus began the meal in the usual way, by blessing the bread and then distributing pieces to the participants in the meal. He accompanied this ritual action with another statement which must have seemed strange: "This is my body." The Romans later suspected the Christians of superstition and abominable practices. The Gospel of John spends chapter six trying to explain the meaning of Jesus' body in the face of rejection by some followers. During Passover, the body of the Passover lamb is eaten. The Passover meal, and all the meals eaten at the Temple by worshipers, were sacrificial meals in which part of the animal sacrificed on the altar was eaten in God's presence as a sign of unity with God and dependence on divine care. Such meals established and secured the relationship between God and humanity. "This is my body" identifies Jesus with the Passover lamb and his death with the sacrifices in the Temple. The meal with his disciples, repeated by Christians since, is a participation in that sacrifice, a meal consisting of the sacrificed victim and taken in the presence of God. Where the sacrifice is, God is. When the meal takes place, humans and God are reconciled and united. The power of Passover, of salvation from death in Egypt, of freedom from death and slavery, is actualized. Each Jew must believe that he/she personally has been saved from Egypt and death; each Christian must believe that he/she has been saved from sin and death.

*The Wine*

The cup of wine would have been taken after the meal, as the third cup of wine in the Passover ritual. Mark does not say that a meal took place between Jesus' blessing of the bread and the wine (Luke and Paul make this clear). The original setting of these symbolic actions and words has fallen away and the memory of Jesus' words has entered the worship of Mark's community. Later liturgical practice and Jewish Passover ritual have influenced Mark's description of what Jesus did at the last meal with his disciples. The cup of wine is designated as Jesus' blood, but with additional explanation: "This is my blood of the covenant which is poured out for many." The sharing of a drink, especially at a meal, is a common symbol of unity and good feeling. Before Jesus gave the cup to his disciples, the Gospel says that he gave thanks. The Greek word for giving thanks is the same as that used for the Church's celebration of Jesus' last supper: Eucharist. Cup can also be a symbol for one's destiny in life, especially suffering. Earlier Jesus responded to James and John, who asked to sit at his side when he came into his glory, by asking them if they could drink the cup he drinks. They bravely and ignorantly replied that they could. The ambiguity of "cup" elucidates the nature of Jesus' activity. When we drink the cup, we are united with Jesus in his sacrificial meal, but we are also united with him in the sacrifice, that is, in the suffering and death endemic to life and necessary to all human endeavor.

Jesus explains the meaning of the wine by an additional phrase: "This is my blood *of the covenant which is poured out for many.*" The covenant is the treaty or agreement made between God and Israel at Mount Sinai when Moses received the Ten Commandments and other laws (Ex 19—24). After Moses descended from the mountain, the people of Israel sacrificed an animal on an altar at the base of the mountain. Moses poured out half of the blood at the base of the altar, a common sacrificial practice, and sprinkled the other half of it over the people. Like Jesus, Moses explains the symbolic meaning of the blood: "Behold the blood of the covenant which the Lord has made with you in accordance with all these words" (Ex 24:8). In addition, Moses and the elders of Israel went up and "beheld God, and ate and drank." All of these activities, both Moses' and Jesus', fit in perfectly with Israelite festivals and ways of relating to God. We relate with God through an agreement which binds us to one another. This agreement or covenant engages our whole selves, our body and blood. God also gives a total guarantee of fidelity, the seriousness of which is symbolized by blood, the stuff of life. For example, in one of the prophets God says: "Because of the blood of my covenant with you, I will set your captives free from the waterless pit" (Zech 9:11). The later Aramaic translation of the Hebrew original (called a Targum) fittingly connects the blood of the covenant, which results in captives being set free, with Passover when the blood of the Passover animal saved Israel from death in Egypt. Jesus' brief and enigmatic words over the wine reach back into this rich stream of tradition and belief in Israel and set his own actions within the larger canvas of God's activity throughout Israel's history. Jesus now comes to save not just Israel, but *all,* for this is the meaning of the Hebrew and Aramaic idiom "many." Jesus is implicitly identified with the Passover and covenant sacrifices in which the body and blood of the victim are symbolically offered to God and which are concluded by a meal of the sacrificial victim shared by humans and God. In a new setting and with modified purpose Jesus and his disciples begin to reenact the Passover and covenant, a reenactment which will be completed with Jesus' death and resurrection.

### The Messianic Banquet

Jesus concludes his ritual explanation with a prediction which introduces the cosmic dimension of the Kingdom of God: "Truly, I say to you, I shall not drink again of the fruit of the vine until that day when I drink it new in the Kingdom of God." This verse reaches into the future the way the previous verse reached into the past. Jesus' final meal and also his death are related to the end time and the coming of God's Kingdom. Jesus' death will not be the end, but the beginning of something new. The drinking of the wine and the eating together do not end with this last meal on earth, but are a foreshadowing of the relationship Jesus' disciples will have with him in the future.

Jesus' reference to drinking in the Kingdom of God recalls a common image in Jewish literature and belief, the Messianic banquet. Both the Bible and other Jewish literature picture those who have been faithful to God ultimately sitting down to a great banquet with him.

> On this mountain the Lord of hosts
> will make for all peoples
> a feast of fat things,
> a feast of wine on the lees,
> of fat things full of marrow,
> of wine on the lees well refined.
> And he will destroy on this mountain
> the covering that is cast over all peoples,
> the veil that is spread over all nations.
> He will swallow up death forever,
> and the Lord God will wipe away tears from all faces,
> and the reproach of his people he will take away
> from all the earth (Is 25:6–8).

This scene was so familiar to first century Jews that Jesus referred to it explicitly when predicting that many non-Jews will enter God's Kingdom: "I tell you, many will come from east and west and sit at table with Abraham, Isaac and Jacob in the Kingdom of heaven" (Mt 8:11). Thus, Jesus' last meal with his disciples recalls both the first Passover when Israel began to exist as a nation and the final meal all will enjoy in God's Kingdom. The link between these two events and the meal Jesus is eating with his disciples is forged by Jesus himself, who is the new Passover sacrifice. Jesus brings the freedom and salvation of the first Passover to completion and brings the Kingdom of God to fulfillment in himself and his actions. Jesus is not only the Passover lamb for his disciples, he is the *eschatological* Passover lamb who brings about the completion of God's work with humanity and the perfection of God's Kingdom at the banquet presided over by the Messiah.

Mark concludes his narration with: "When they had sung a hymn, they went out to the Mount of Olives." The hymn may have been the Hallel, the great hymn of praise and thanksgiving to God sung at Passover and in the Temple worship. Jesus' words and action, as important as they are for Christians, take place in a Jewish setting and in the context of worship of God, a worship carried on by Jews for well over a thousand years before Jesus lived. Jesus himself, and his work and his significance, grow and draw sustinence from the God of Israel known through Israel's traditions and faith. Passover is one of these traditional feasts. Though the Gospel of Mark tells the story of Jesus' last evening with his disciples briefly and simply, each phrase and each action draws upon the wealth of Jewish tradition and the depth of Jewish faith. What Jesus did and what he accomplished cannot be known from a meal and his death alone. Only someone steeped in God's word and work in the Bible can understand and believe that Jesus' death saves. Mark explains this paradox using the imagery and symbols of Passover with its sacrifice and meal.

## The Gospel of Matthew

Matthew's traditions concerning Jesus and Passover came from Mark, so we will focus on Matthew's special themes. He stresses Jesus' sovereign control over his own destiny and the self-giving implied in his actions. Even though Jesus is arrested, condemned to death and executed, he remains in control of his life. He knows what will happen and acquiesces to it. Jesus' purpose in sacrificing himself emerges clearly, to bring about forgiveness of sins. Jesus, the Son of God, endures the passion and death, but his majesty and power lurk near the surface.

*Context*

Like Mark, Matthew prefaces the story of Jesus' death with a description of the end of the world. In the second half (24:37—25:46) Matthew exhorts Christians to a life of love and mercy while they wait for Jesus' coming. A number of striking parables carry his message and the last of them includes several themes (25:31–46). As Jesus is judging humankind, he orders the sheep to his right hand and the goats to his left. The sheep he invites into God's Kingdom and the goats he condemns to eternal fire. The basis for this separation is one's attitude toward Jesus: Did one care for Jesus when he was hungry, thirsty, naked, sick and imprisoned? Each group asks Jesus when they did this or failed to do it for him and Jesus answers that when they did it to any one of the least of his brethren they did it to him.

Several things stand out in this scene of judgment. Jesus appears in his full glory and power. "When the Son of man comes in his glory, and all the angels with him, then he will sit on his glorious throne. Before him will be gathered all the nations. . . ." The scene shows that Jesus, who soon will be powerless, suffer and die, will in the end conquer his enemies. He who appears ordinary and even oppressed possesses supreme power. In Jesus heaven and earth, the human and the divine, unite. Jesus' death and resurrection are as important, effective and significant as the judgment at the end of the world, for the central figure in each is the same. The new age of the Christian community, inaugurated by Jesus in pain, will be concluded by him in glory. Humans do not take their place in this scene by doing anything esoteric or achieving any great insight. They gain their destiny the same way Jesus did—by mercifully loving fellow human beings and by suffering patiently the problems and persecutions inherent in Christian life. Thus Matthew prepares us to understand Jesus by showing us his true self and our true call as believers. The reader is now prepared to identify with Jesus as he enters the final, crucial hours of his life.

*Passover*

Jesus himself begins his passion by telling his disciples: "You know that after two days the Passover is coming, and the Son of man will be delivered up to be crucified." Passover and Jesus' crucifixion go together in God's plan. Jesus knows the truth and accepts God's will. He refers to himself as the Son of man, the same symbolic figure who appeared gloriously in the preceding scene. His suffering and glory go together, just as the sacrifice and salvation of Passover go together. Later when Jesus sends his disciples to get a room for the Passover meal, they are ordered to tell the house owner that Jesus says: "My time is at hand; I will keep the Passover at your house with my disciples" (26:18). Jesus' time to die and the feast of Passover are the same. Jesus does not *request* a room, but *states* that he will use it. He is not uncertain about his future, but declares what it will be. Jesus orchestrates his own end in Matthew; like the Son of man at the final judgment, he remains in control and brings all to completion.

Matthew follows Mark in the description of Jesus' final meal but adds a couple of important explanations. When blessing the cup, Jesus says that it is his "blood of the covenant which is poured out for many *for the forgiveness of sins.*" The precise result of Jesus' death and the covenant with God is the forgiving of sins. Just as the sacrifices in the Temple atoned for sins and the Passover lamb saved the Israelites from death, Jesus' self-sacrifice saves believers from sin through bringing about their forgiveness. Matthew forshadowed this when the angel said to Joseph that Jesus would "save his people from their sins" (1:21). That forgiveness is linked to Jesus' death and also to the celebration of the Lord's supper, the memorial of his death.

When speaking of the final Messianic banquet, Jesus says he will not drink wine "until that day when I drink it new *with you* in *my Father's Kingdom.*" The intimate relationship among Jesus, his followers and his Father are emphasized just as the caring and loving relationships among followers of Jesus were stressed in the judgment scene. Passover with his disciples gains depth and scope through reference to Israel's past and the Church's future which are held together by the one God of Israel who is Jesus' Father and the one Son of man who dies and rises, suffers and judges.

## The Gospel of Luke

Luke stresses the pilgrimages made by Jesus, journeys out of ordinary life toward God. God's purpose in history, the connections between Jesus' and Israel's history and the present history of the Church are intertwined with the Passover meals of Israel, of Jesus and of the Christian worship. Remembering God who is good and Jesus who sacrifices himself should produce patient endurance in adversity. Jesus, the model of endurance, has an especially close relationship to his disciples.

## Jesus' Youth

The first two chapters of Luke, which concern the birth and childhood of Jesus, contain many hints of what will follow during the ministry and passion of Jesus. In the last incident of the prologue the twelve year old Jesus accompanies his parents on their pilgrimage to the Temple to celebrate Passover (2:41–50). At the end of the week-long festival Jesus' parents begin traveling back to Galilee without realizing that Jesus is absent from the caravan. When they search Jerusalem, they find him "in the Temple, sitting among the teachers, listening to them and asking them questions." Jesus explains the worry he caused them by the enigmatic question: "Did you not know that I must be in my Father's house (or about my Father's business)?"

This youthful Passover resembles Jesus' final Passover in several ways. In Luke 9:51 Jesus "set his face to go to Jerusalem." He arrives there in chapter 19 and experiences the events leading to his death. The story of Jesus' first youthful journey to Jerusalem foreshadows his final adult journey. Both journeys are pilgrimages to celebrate Passover. A pilgrimage is a journey made to a holy place in order to engage in some special kind of worship. It requires that the believer leave the ordinary things of life and devote full energy to God. The old patterns are broken, and new, more intimate ways of relating to God replace them.

For Luke the Temple and Jerusalem are central to God's revelation and to Jesus' life and work. Jesus goes to Jerusalem to die and rise, and from Jerusalem the early Christian community spreads until it reaches Rome at the end of the Acts of the Apostles (Luke's second volume). As a boy Jesus goes to the Temple and interacts with the teachers of Judaism. Even in his youth Jesus has wisdom and can interpret the law and the prophets; later he will enter into controversy with the Jewish leaders and teach authoritatively himself. Jesus himself is God's revelation and God's authoritative interpreter, something hinted at by the story of his unusual discussions with the teachers. Jesus' mother reproaches him for causing her and her husband pain: "Son, why have you treated us so?" But Jesus' unusual action in stay-ing behind either to be about his Father's business or to be in his Father's house (the Greek original can have both meanings) hints at his ultimate des-tiny which is to suffer and be separated from family and disciples by death. Though no explicit mention is made of Jesus' suffering in the narrative of his first Passover, his Passover dedication to his Father, his experience of pil-grimage as separation from family and his activity at the Temple during the Passover feast look forward to the last Passover at the end of Luke's Gospel.

### The Last Passover

After Jesus' final discourse concerning the end of the world and the de-struction of Jerusalem, Luke summarizes his activity around Jerusalem dur-ing his last Passover as follows: "And every day he was teaching in the temple, but at night he went out and lodged on the mount called Olivet. And early in the morning all the people came to him in the temple to hear him" (21:37–38). As he was in his youth so he is at the height of his career. Jesus teaches in Jerusalem, the center of Judaism, and in the Temple, God's house. He is not at home in Jerusalem, but a pilgrim there to worship God at Passover. He will soon leave Jerusalem to return to his Father. Yet Jeru-salem and the religion of Israel centered at the Temple are important and even crucial to Jesus' work and death. He teaches as a Jewish teacher at the center of Judaism. He sacrifices himself at the place where Jewish sacrifices are offered to God and at a feast which celebrates Judaism's escape from death and pilgrimage through the desert to freedom and life.

Luke strongly emphasizes God's purpose during Passover by using a key word in his opening line: "Then came the day of Unleavened Bread, on which the Passover *had to be sacrificed*" (22:7). The expression "had to" or more literally "it was necessary" is used often by Luke to signify what God has willed and planned for Jesus or for humanity. The "Passover" means the Passover sacrifice and in this case the word has double meaning because "the Passover" means both the ordinary Passover sacrifices and Jesus him-self who will be sacrificed. In the first Passover God commanded the Israel-ites to sacrifice an animal and mark their doorposts with its blood so that the angel of death would not kill their first-born sons along with the Egyptians'. God also demanded that the Jews remember and recreate this event each year on a set day in the month of Nisan. In the same way God asks that Jesus sacrifice himself at this Passover and that his followers remember his sacrifice in the Lord's supper. Luke connects the Passover sacrifices with Jesus' last meal with the expression "When the hour came" (22:14). The time of the Passover feast with its sacrifices, the time of the meal, and the time of Jesus' own sacrifice of himself have all been set by God and accepted by Jesus. All form one complex reality which gathers up the past and points to the future within the rich and holy time of Passover.

Luke parallels Jesus' close relationship with his Father to his special relationship with his disciples. When Jesus arranges to celebrate the Passover, he tells Peter and John: "Go and prepare the Passover *for us,* that we may eat it." The phrase "for us" is not found in Matthew and Mark. Jesus' love for his disciples becomes more explicitly clear when Jesus begins the meal by telling the apostles: "I have earnestly desired to eat this Passover with you before I suffer" (22:15). Passover, suffering, the meal and Jesus' followers are inextricably bound to one another and to Jesus. Jesus becomes the Passover sacrifice and Jesus' love for his disciples demands that they remain faithful to him and endure persecution and suffering on his behalf.

## The Meal

The Gospel of Luke has a number of traditions concerning the passion, death and resurrection of Jesus which are not found in the other Gospels. For example, Luke tells the story of Jesus' giving his disciples the bread and wine twice (22:15–18 and 19–20). The first account stresses the link between this meal and the future Messianic banquet. The second, in which he says "This is my body. . . . This is my blood," is similar to the liturgical formula found in Paul's First Letter to the Corinthians and comes from the worship service familiar to Luke from his community. The presence of two descriptions, though it seems odd at first, succeeds in identifying three meals with one another: Jesus' meal, the meal celebrated by the Christian community and the final meal in God's Kingdom. Luke, who continued his Gospel with a second volume (Acts of the Apostles) describing the early Christian community, often links the life and teachings of Jesus with the community life of the later Church. Jesus' intimate union with his followers demonstrates how the members of the community should love one another.

Jesus' willingness to sacrifice and suffer adversity in order to carry out God's will urges believers to fidelity to God and the community worship and to patient endurance of hardship in Jesus' name. The final meal in God's Kingdom flows from the community's meal together and it itself reenacts Jesus' own last meal and sacrifice. More than the other Gospel writers Luke sets Jesus and his deeds within history. But he does not present history as a series of isolated events; the beginning, the end and the high points of history all fit together in God's plan.

Jesus indicates the importance of this Passover with his disciples when he tells them: "I shall not eat it until it is fulfilled in the Kingdom of God." "It" seems to refer to the Passover sacrifice. The fulfillment of the Passover in this instance requires that the real Passover sacrifice, Jesus, be sacrificed and enter God's Kingdom. Then at the Messianic banquet he will again eat with his followers. There may also be a reference to the meal Jesus' followers eat with him and one another when they worship, that is, the Eucharist. When Jesus gives them the cup he says: "I tell you that from now on I shall not drink of the fruit of the vine until the Kingdom of God comes" (22:18). The coming of the Kingdom can refer both to the time after Jesus' resurrection and to the end of the world. Thus the life of the Church and life in the Kingdom become associated and partially identified. The celebration of Passover in Jesus' life, the celebration of Jesus as the Passover sacrifice in the Eucharist and the celebration of the saved in the Kingdom of God all take place with Jesus as the symbolic center and focus of meaning.

## The Eucharist

The formulae which Luke quotes from the worship of his Church community contain several particulars not found in Mark and Matthew. Jesus' sacrifice is made explicit when Jesus says: "This is my body *which is given for you*" (22:19). A body which is given for another recalls the Temple sacrifices. Luke continues: "Do this in remembrance of me." Remembering is central to the Passover feast. The participants in the Passover meal retell the story of the original Passover, instruct their young in its meaning and identify with the story so that they themselves become the ones saved from Pharaoh in Egypt. Likewise, Christians identify with Jesus and his Passover sacrifice in such a way that they are saved from sin. The Church community remembers Jesus' Passover meal and sacrifice as effectively as the Jewish community remembers the Passover in Exodus. The spirit of both celebrations is captured well by a prayer sung after the meal in the Passover Seder:

Our God and God of our Fathers,
may there rise and come and approach,
and be seen, accepted, heard, recollected and remembered
the remembrance of us and the recollection of us,
and the remembrance of our fathers,
and the remembrance of the Messiah, son of David, your servant,
and the remembrance of Jerusalem, your holy city,
and the remembrance of all your people, the house of Israel.
May their remembrance come before you for life and for peace
on this the Festival of Unleavened Bread.

Many of the beliefs and figures remembered and the things prayed for in the Jewish community have been transferred to the Christian community and associated with Jesus. Messiah, salvation, God's people, Jerusalem and all of Israel's history find meaning in Jesus and in the meal Jesus left his followers.

"And likewise the cup *after supper.* . . ." Luke's liturgical formula for the blessing of the bread and wine preserves the original setting of these actions at a meal. Luke understands the meal as a Passover meal. The third cup was drunk after the participants ate and Jesus gave it new meaning: "This cup which is poured out for you is the *new* covenant in my blood." The pouring of the cup recalls the pouring of the sacrificial blood at the base of the altar in the covenant ceremony at Mount Sinai (Ex 24). But this is a new covenant. Luke shows great respect for Israel and for the Jewish traditions and takes great pains to show that Christianity stands in continuity with Israel. However, believers in Jesus have a new covenant, a new relationship with God. The prophet Jeremiah spoke of such a covenant six hundred years earlier when Jerusalem and the Temple had been destroyed and all seemed lost for Israel:

Behold, the days are coming, says the Lord,
when I will make a new covenant

with the house of Israel and the house of Judah,
not like the covenant which I made with their fathers
when I took them by the hand
to bring them out of the land of Egypt,
my covenant which they broke,
though I was their husband, says the Lord.
But this is the covenant which I will make
with the house of Israel after those days, says the Lord;
I will put my law within them,
and I will write it upon their hearts;
and I will be their God
and they shall be my people (Jer 31:31–33).

Luke alludes to this passage in referring to the covenant that Jesus makes as a *new* covenant. Notice the intimacy between God and his people. In Jeremiah God's law will be within them in the same way that the Spirit is within Christians in Luke–Acts.

The blessing over the cup is followed with a prediction that Jesus will be betrayed. There is no pause nor any change of scene. "But behold the hand of him who betrays me is with me on the table." Luke balances his stress on table fellowship with an awareness that members of the community can be unfaithful to Jesus and to their fellow believers. Both in Jesus' time and in Luke's the danger of apostasy or of weakness in the face of opposition plagued the community. The Passover meal, with its background of danger and salvation in Egypt and its more immediate relationship to Jesus' own death, symbolizes both God's power and human evil. Weakness must be overcome by the Passover sacrifice which Jesus makes and by the meal that brings the power of that sacrifice to the participant.

A series of instructions follow the supper. Jesus prepares his disciples to understand what he will do and to endure the fear and pain which will follow. First he connects the promise of a heavenly banquet to perseverance in the way that he goes.

You are those who have continued with me in my trials; and I assign to you, as my Father assigns to me, a kingdom, that you may eat and drink at my table in my kingdom, and sit on thrones judging the twelve tribes of Israel (22:28–30).

In an earlier parable Luke connected the heavenly banquet with feeding the poor and needy and with responding to God's invitation (14:12–24). But at the critical moment of Jesus' suffering, endurance is paramount.

The nature of Christian life after Jesus' death and resurrection can be seen in the last paragraph of Jesus' instructions. Jesus reminds them that he sent them out to preach (chapter 10) without any money or clothing. Now he tells them to go forth equipped with those things and a sword also. This change in instruction symbolizes the time following Jesus' departure from the earth when his followers, the Church, will be oppressed and struggle to survive. The meal, which remembers what Jesus did, will remain at the center of the community, but the community's relations with the outside world will be troubled, just as the original Passover meal bound the Hebrews together in Egypt despite the threat to their existence from Pharaoh.

## The Gospel of John

The Gospel of John immediately stands out from the other Gospels because of its different content and its symbolic and repetitive style. The author of John tells fewer stories about Jesus but explains them using lengthy dialogues or discourses in which Jesus teaches the meaning of what he does. Symbols repeated throughout the Gospel give depth to Jesus' actions. Though John has some materials in common with the other Gospels, he also has a varied fund of unique early traditions.

Passover and Passover symbols are frequent and central in John. John the Baptist proclaims Jesus as the "Lamb of God, who takes away the sin of the world" (1:29). Lamb symbolism is used often in the Old Testament prophets for Israel and is used of Jesus at the end of the world in Revelation, where Jesus is the Lamb who was slain. Both in John, chapter one, and in Revelation the Lamb of God is identified with the suffering servant portrayed in Isaiah, chapter 53. In John the Lamb of God is said to take away the sin of the world. The lamb reminds us of all the sacrifices for sin offered at the Temple. The prominence of Passover in John suggests a special allusion to the Passover sacrifice.

John alludes to the first Passover and to the Hebrews' escape from Egypt under Moses' leadership often. In the prologue (1:14) the Word comes and dwells, literally "tents," with us. This recalls the tent of meeting where God appeared to Moses in the desert. In chapter three Jesus refers to the bronze serpent which Moses raised up for the people to see in the desert so that they could be cured of the plague of poisonous snakes and saved from death. Jesus is compared to Moses at various times (1:17; 5:45–47; 6:31). Both he and Moses do signs and are disbelieved when they have had contact with God's glory. The manna eaten in the desert (6:31) and the water which came from a rock there (7:38–39) also figure in Jesus' discourses.

Jesus experiences three Passovers in John's narrative. (Because of the mention of three Passovers, writers of the life of Jesus have said that his ministry lasted three years.) The first and last Passovers are celebrated in Jerusalem at the beginning and end of his public life. The middle Passover is really the period just before Passover when Jesus speaks about himself as the bread of life (chapter 6). Each Passover is the setting for major activities and teachings related to Jesus' death and its effect on his followers and the world. Each Passover results in both belief and disbelief among those who have contact with Jesus.

## The First Passover

At the beginning of chapter two Jesus does the first of seven "signs" in Cana of Galilee when he turns water into wine at a wedding feast. Signs are unusual and wonderful deeds (miracles) which symbolize what will happen to Jesus and what lies beyond the obvious and physical. (In the Synoptic Gospels most miracles are deeds of power which defeat evil and help establish God's Kingdom; in John they are more prophecy and symbol for what will be.) The wedding feast is a meal which recalls Jesus' last supper and the Messianic banquet of the future age. The water turned into wine fits in the same context. In chapter six, Jesus speaks of eating his body and drinking his blood when he multiplies the loaves of bread for the people. All these symbols exist on several temporal levels, the present Passover feast, the time of Jesus' death and the future Kingdom of God.

Immediately after this first sign, Jesus goes to Jerusalem to celebrate the Passover. In the Temple he found people selling sacrificial animals and changing money into coins that could be used for offerings in the Temple. These people would have been located in the porticoes and in the ample open spaces around the Temple. Jesus drives them out, quoting a psalm that the Temple should not be a place for commerce. This challenge to the people doing business is odd. We saw earlier that commerce was quite acceptable in the Temple precincts and even necessary for people who wished to offer sacrifices. But Jesus' cleansing of the Temple points to something beyond the everyday life of Judaism and its worship in the Temple.

The prophetic verse used to describe the activity of John the Baptist continues in a way which describes Jesus' activity here:

> Behold, I send my messenger
>     to prepare the way before me,
> *and the Lord whom you seek*
>     *will suddenly come to his temple:*
> the messenger of the covenant in whom you delight,
>     behold, he is coming (Mal 3:1).

The cleansing of the Temple from human imperfection which might taint it is a common sign of the Messianic age when God's messenger will suddenly come and justice will prevail. For example, the later more apocalyptic part of Zechariah ends (14:21):

> And every pot in Jerusalem and Judah
>     shall be sacred to the Lord of hosts,
> so that all who sacrifice may come and take of them
>     and boil the flesh of the sacrifice in them.
> *And there shall no longer be a trader*
>     *in the house of the Lord of hosts on that day.*

Criticism of what went on in the Temple was common to the prophets centuries earlier. For example, Jeremiah said: "Has this house, which is called by my name, become a den of robbers in your eyes?" (7:11). The explanation given by John for Jesus' actions is contained in a psalm: "Zeal for your house has consumed me and the insults of those who insult you have fallen on me" (Ps 69:9). Note that the second half of the verse looks forward to the time that Jesus will be rejected and killed.

Jesus is challenged by the authorities in the Temple who ask for a sign of his own authority. The sign he gives is a symbolic saying: "Destroy this temple, and in three days I will raise it up" (2:19). Temple, of course, refers both to the physical temple and to Jesus' body which will die and rise. Jesus here and often in John replaces Jewish institutions with his actions and his teachings. The promise to build a Temple which it took forty-six years to build hints at the eschatological Temple which God will provide for worship at the end, a Temple without human imperfections.

John ends Jesus' stay in Jerusalem with the observation that many who saw the signs which Jesus did believed in him. Jesus, however, did not trust himself to this type of believer because this faith was based on awe at his powerful deeds and not on real apprehension of who Jesus was and what he could do to save the world. As the Gospel goes on, the struggle between real, deep faith and superficial fascination with Jesus will become clear.

Caution toward people who lack faith continues when Jesus arrives back in Galilee. The Galileans who have seen all that he did at the Passover feast welcome him, but Jesus testifies that "a prophet has no honor in his own country" (4:43–45). Jesus returns to Cana, where he turned water into wine as his first sign. There a Gentile official from Capernaum begs him to heal his son and believes that Jesus has the power to do this even at a distance. This cure is Jesus' second sign, and the faith of the non-Jew in Jesus further shows the power of his symbolic acts, but also their limits. "Unless you see signs and wonders you will not believe" (4:48). More faith will be required at the next Passover when Jesus speaks of himself as the bread of life and some will reject him.

In the early chapters of John the theme of life is intertwined with that of faith. Jesus gives wine, one of the nutrients of life, to the people at Cana. He speaks to Nicodemus about being born again of water and the Holy Spirit (chapter 3). He speaks of living water giving eternal life to the Samaritan woman (chapter 4) and he cures both the official's son and the paralytic by the pool of Bethzatha in Jerusalem (chapter 5). This theme of life continues into chapter six where Jesus multiplies a few loaves to feed five thousand people and then teaches them that he is the bread of life.

*The Second Passover*

Chapters five to ten in John are held together by a sequence of Jewish feasts. Jesus engages in his works and preaching on the Sabbath and at the feasts of Passover, Pentecost and Booths. By revealing God anew in this context he revalues and replaces these Jewish liturgical practices with himself and his teaching. The true believer in Jesus is asked to move from the historical reality of Judaism to the true heavenly reality revealed by and present in Jesus.

In chapter six the season is spring, a time of growth, life and harvest in the Middle East. Jesus teaches a large crowd which follows him into the hills at the edge of the Sea of Galilee. Jesus tells his disciples to feed the approximately five thousand people sitting on the grass with a few loaves, and the bread suffices. Feeding in the wilderness where there is no food reminds us of the manna which God gave to the Hebrews when they were in the desert after escaping from Egypt. The hills recall the mountain in the wilderness where God revealed himself to his people.

The people's reaction brings up the problem of faith based on signs again:

> When the people saw the sign which he had done, they said, "This is indeed the prophet who is to come into the world." Perceiving then that they were about to come and take him by force to make him king, Jesus withdrew again to the hills by himself (6:14–15).

The people see Jesus as a powerful political leader and think that the Messianic age has come. The expectation that God's chosen messenger (in some sources, a prophet) will come to bring justice and freedom is especially alive in the popular imagination during the Passover feast. One of the tasks of John's Gospel is to demonstrate that the ordinary expectations of the people are incorrect. For example, during his trial Jesus tells Pilate that he is a king, but his Kingdom is not of this world. Jesus is a king in an unusual sense and lacks all the defensive power and trappings of royalty. Yet he truly rules.

Jesus begins his instruction of the people the next day when he tells them that they seek him because they have eaten their fill. Instead they should labor for "the food which endures to eternal life." When they ask what they must do, Jesus once again brings up the problem of faith: "This is the work of God, that you believe in him whom he has sent" (6:29). They predictably ask him what sign he performs and bring up as an example the manna which their ancestors ate in the wilderness. Jesus responds that it was not Moses but God who gave them bread from heaven, and now the Father gives them "the true bread from heaven. For the bread of God is that which comes down from heaven, and gives life to the world" (6:33–34).

The people unwittingly begin the next and most difficult stage of instruction when they ask that Jesus give them this bread always. Jesus answers: "I am the bread of life; he who comes to me shall not hunger, and he who believes in me shall never thirst. . . . For I have come down from heaven. . . . This is the will of the Father, that everyone who sees the Son and believes in him should have eternal life. . . ." This series of metaphoric and symbolic statements goes far beyond the simple reality of being fed on a hillside or the even more complex experience of eating manna in the desert. The listeners are being challenged to understand Jesus' activity on a more than literal level. But since they have only responded to the feeding and to the simple reality of Jesus' signs, they do not understand and begin to grumble and question.

Jesus goes on instructing the people and ironically they understand less. A believer must move beyond the physical realities of life if he/she is to understand Jesus' life, message and very self. Jesus is a heavenly figure who has come to earth, and the realities which he communicates are beyond our ordinary knowledge and perception. Jesus summarizes and deepens his teaching:

> I am the bread of life.
> Your fathers ate manna in the wilderness, and they died.
> This is the bread which comes down from heaven,
> that a man may eat of it and not die.
> I am the living bread which came down from heaven;
> if anyone eats of this bread, he will live forever;
> and the bread which I shall give for the life of the world
> is my flesh (6:48–51).

The final clause, that the bread is Jesus' flesh, causes another uproar. Of course, to John's readers in his late first century community, Jesus' whole discourse points to their celebration of the Christian Eucharist where the bread and wine are Jesus' body and blood. This later awareness is built into the life of Jesus and his teaching and communicates a terrible irony. Those who do not really understand Jesus and believe in him cannot be members of the Christian community because they cannot eat the body and blood of the Lord at the community's meal. Only believers can participate in the community when it obeys the commands of the Lord. Jesus' final explanation makes even more explicit the connection between his teaching on the bread of life and the community's Eucharist: "Unless you eat the flesh of the Son of man and drink his blood, you have no life in you; he who eats my flesh and drinks my blood has eternal life, and I will raise him up on the last day" (6:53–54).

Eating and drinking Jesus' body and blood could suggest some sort of cannibalism and Christians have occasionally been accused of this. However, to a Jewish ear of the first century, eating and drinking in a ceremonial context suggest a sacrifice at the Temple and the subsequent meal in which the worshipers ate part of the victim in God's house. Here Jesus speaks just before the Passover feast in the spring and his words link sacrifice, bread and life with God and the one whom God sent, himself. All of these themes can be found in Exodus in the story of the first Passover and in the Passover ritual of Jesus' day. John simply constructs a discourse which catches all these themes and connotations in order to communicate Jesus' message concerning his relation to the Father, his work on earth and the response we should make.

Of course, the people reject Jesus, as do some of his disciples. Jesus then asks the twelve if they will leave, too, and Peter responds: "Lord, to whom shall we go? You have the words of eternal life; and we have believed and have come to know, that you are the Holy One of God" (6:68–69). Though the disciples do not fully understand Jesus, they do know that he is from beyond their daily experience and that in this special place God and life are found.

The Johannine teaching that Jesus has come from the Father in heaven and returns to him and that he brings life through his sacrifice stretches the listener's imagination. Only by a massive use of metaphor and symbolism in the rich context of Passover is John able to suggest the real meaning of Jesus.

*The Last Passover*

Strangely John's account of Jesus' last meal does not speak of his words over the bread and wine. Perhaps because John has developed this teaching in chapter six, at the time of the previous Passover, he omits it here. Instead he tells the story of Jesus washing his disciples' feet, a foreshadowing of his humiliation and death for their sakes; and then a discourse five chapters long prepares Jesus' disciples for his death and life without him on earth.

The supper Jesus has with his disciples is not a Passover meal because the next day, on which he is crucified, is the preparation day for the Passover (18:28). Though John does not adopt the expedient of the other Gospels by identifying the meal with a Passover meal (and he is probably historically correct in this), he does identify Jesus with the lambs sacrificed for the Passover meal. Jesus is finally condemned by Pilate at the sixth hour of the day, that is, at noon (19:14) and so he dies on the cross during the afternoon while the Passover animals are being sacrificed at the Temple. The real Lamb of God who takes away the sins of the world is on the cross, not in the Temple. The old has been replaced by the new.

The theme of newness can be found in the final discourse of Jesus with his disciples. Jesus says near the beginning: "A *new* commandment I give to you, that you love one another" (13:34). The command to love is repeated twice more (15:12, 17) and is central to Jesus' final teaching. The reference to a new commandment recalls the new covenant prophesied by Jeremiah (31:31). Commandments have force only within a covenant between God and humans. Again, Jesus is replacing a Jewish institution with himself and his teaching. He is now the transmitter and guarantor of the covenant, for he is greater than Moses.

Allusions to the first Passover sacrifice give depth to John's description of Jesus' death. Just as Jesus is about to die, someone puts a sponge dipped in vinegar on the end of a branch of hyssop and holds it up to Jesus. Hyssop is a common shrub in the Middle East, and the Book of Exodus says that the Hebrews used hyssop branches to smear their doorposts with the blood of the Passover sacrifice so that the angel of death would pass them by (Ex 12:22). After Jesus dies, the soldiers come around to break his legs and hasten his death. When they see that he is dead, they do not break his legs. John explains that this was to fulfill Scripture: "Not a bone of his shall be broken" (Jn 19:36 quoting Ex 12:46). The Passover regulations included a command that no bones of the sacrificial animal were to be broken, and this regulation is observed at this Passover in which the ultimate Passover lamb has been sacrificed.

Why has John told this story? For what purpose has he reached back into Israel's history to Passover and assembled so many other symbols besides?

> Now Jesus did many other signs in the presence of the disciples, which are not written in this book; but these are written that you may believe that Jesus is the Christ, the Son of God, and that believing you may have life in his name (20:30–31).

John has joined life and faith which come from God, the experience of Israel at the first Passover, Jesus' self-sacrifice at his last Passover, and the celebration of Passover carried on each time the believing community gathers to eat Jesus' flesh and drink his blood. His elaborate presentation of Jesus promotes a deeper and more adequate understanding of and faith in Jesus.

# 6

# *Passover in Other New Testament Writings*

Several early Christian writings beside the Gospels mention or allude to the Passover lamb. The meaning and relevance of Passover for Christians are taken for granted and put to use for literary, theological and ethical purposes. Within a couple of decades after Jesus' death he was firmly identified with Passover and all its symbolism. The richness of the Passover imagery recommended it to Christians as a way of understanding Jesus. The centrality of Passover and the Exodus to Jewish ideas of redemption and salvation provided a model for Christian reflection on Jesus as the final Savior sent by God.

Because it is a powerful symbol, Passover influences the way life is lived by Christians and suggests practical conclusions for the attitudes and behavioral patterns which characterize Christianity. The Exodus story, in which God saved the Hebrews from slavery and death in Egypt, has always provided a pattern for God's saving of Christians from sin through Jesus Christ. The blood of the Passover lamb which kept God from killing the first-born children of the Hebrews suggests the blood of Jesus shed on the cross and symbolically offered and consumed in the liturgy. Jesus himself is the Passover lamb in Christianity. The cleaning out of old leaven at the beginning of the feast of Unleavened Bread naturally suggests moral reform as do the ritual purity and sacrifices for sin associated with the Temple. Both the Israelite participation in Passover and the Christian participation in Jesus' sacrifice rest upon a lively faith and a willing obedience to God. We will review several uses of Passover symbolism, beginning with the clearest reference to Passover in Paul's First Letter to the Corinthians.

## The First Letter to the Corinthians

In the course of an admonition to the Corinthian Christian community Paul argues that they should adhere to correct moral behavior because "Christ, our Passover offering, has been sacrificed" (1 Cor 5:7). Paul does not explain this allusion nor does he defend its relevance. He tosses off this identification of Christ with the Passover sacrifice as something well known and accepted among the Corinthians. This is all the more remarkable because the Christian community in Corinth was heavily Gentile. All Christians, not just Christians with Jewish backgrounds, had experienced the power of Passover.

In his First Letter to the Corinthians Paul argued with different factions within the community concerning a variety of issues. Evidently community unity and Christian practice were far from clear and agreed among the newly converted followers of Jesus. In chapter five Paul begins his treatment of specific problems with the most flagrant offense, a son living with his stepmother after his father has died. The Corinthian Christians have done nothing to stop or expel this person and so they condone behavior "of a kind that is not found even among the pagans." Paul is shocked that the Corinthians are arrogant and boast about allowing this behavior, perhaps because they mistakenly concluded that their new freedom in Christ allowed this.

To bring the Corinthians back to reality Paul refers to the feast of Passover and Unleavened Bread as a model for what the community should be.

Do you not know that a little leaven leavens the whole lump? Cleanse out the old leaven that you may be a new lump, as you really are unleavened. For our passover offering has been sacrificed—Christ. Let us therefore celebrate the festival, not with the old leaven, the leaven of malice and evil, but with the unleavened bread of sincerity and truth (1 Cor 5:6–8).

The Christian community which celebrates Passover with Jesus as the Passover sacrifice must engage in behavior appropriate to the Passover festival. Contact with Christ as Redeemer at Passover demands a new way of life. The old, the sinful must be cleaned out of the community the way that old leaven is removed from Jewish homes before Passover begins. The new period initiated by Passover demands new, unleavened, pure bread. Similarly the new Christian community is *really unleavened,* but it must act that way. The nature of the community which celebrates Passover coincides with the nature of Passover. If the community at Corinth has allowed the man living with his stepmother to continue as a member of the community, it has allowed, old, leavened, evil behavior to continue. And this "leaven of malice and evil," even though it is only "a little leaven, leavens the whole lump." Just as Temple rituals must be celebrated in a state of ritual purity, Christian life must be lived in a state of moral purity.

Passover and its customs serve as a model for Christian community and life because Jesus Christ stands at the middle of Passover. Christians should eagerly clean out the old leaven and zealously guard their pure, unleavened state in preparation for Passover because the Passover victim which forms the climax of the Passover meal is ready to be consumed. That sacrificial victim ready for consumption is, of course, Christ. The Passover meal celebrated by Christians as their main act of worship remembers the death and resurrection of Jesus who is now available to the community in the new Passover, the Eucharist. The Gospel interpretation of Jesus' death and resurrection through the Passover feast is presumed and expanded by Paul. As Jews prepare their houses for Passover each year, Christians must prepare their community. The Christian Passover is daily since Jesus is constantly present to the community as its sacrificed Victim and Savior.

Elsewhere in First Corinthians Paul uses images related to Jewish worship in a similar way. While exhorting the Corinthian community to unity against divisive and destructive competition Paul asks them: "Do you (plural) not know that you are God's temple and that God's Spirit dwells in you? If anyone destroys God's temple, God will destroy him. For God's temple is holy, and that temple you are" (3:16–17). Just as the Temple in Jerusalem demands ritual and moral purity from those who participate in its services, the community is now God's temple with God's spirit within it. To destroy in any way this community built by God and his servants will bring a reaction from God.

Later Paul urges restraint because their bodies are members of Christ. In particular, people are to avoid sexual sins because they are a sin against their bodies which have been joined to Christ. A person cannot be one with Christ and with a prostitute both. Paul then characterizes salvation through the temple image: "Do you not know that your body is a temple of the Holy Spirit within you, which you have from God? You are not your own; you were bought with a price. So glorify God in your body" (6:19–20). The moral standards of the community and its members must be modeled on the strict norms for ritual purity and ethical behavior found in the Old Testament laws concerning the Temple. The Temple and its festivals symbolize the new and less tangible structures and relationships which characterize and hold together the Christian community.

In chapter five Paul does not explicitly refer to the Eucharistic meal when he calls Christ our Passover, but he may assume it as a context. Later in chapter eleven he explicitly adjudicates problems which have arisen within the community Eucharistic celebration. One scholar speculates that Paul may be alluding to or implying the existence of a Christian Passover meal celebrated each spring. Even if there was no Passover celebration, Paul is calling upon the Passover tradition to give meaning and guidance to Christian life and community. Behavior in the Eucharistic celebration and in social relations must be consistent.

Jesus, the Passover sacrifice, is called Christ, a common Pauline designation. Christ, the Greek word for Messiah, carries with it another group of associations. The Messiah, the anointed one, will rule God's Kingdom, bring justice and destroy evil at the end. For Paul Jesus the Messiah is also present to the community now and has saved the community through his death and resurrection. Consequently, the Passover sacrifice which has been prepared for the community in Jesus' death and resurrection is unique and final. The community which participates in this Passover is not just saved from Egyptian slavery or other human difficulties, but saved from all evil and sin. Such a community must acknowledge the gifts given it by God and respond with behavior which manifests what God has done in Jesus Christ.

Paul's reference to Passover evokes the Old Testament ideas of sacrifice and ritual holiness. Sacrifices sealed the covenant in Exodus 24 and continued to symbolize Israel's relationship to God while the Temple stood. Sacrifices were offered to glorify God, to expiate sin and to ask for God's help. The Passover sacrifice which is unique in Jewish worship celebrates God's protection of Israel from death and oppression and also his continuing care for them. (See 1 Corinthians 10 where Paul uses the Exodus in another connection.) In Christianity God's salvation is also directed against sin which separates us from God.

Sacrifices offered at the Temple had to be offered by priests and people in a state of ritual purity. The complex biblical rules for ritual purity need not concern us in detail here. The careful ritual preparation for worshiping God reflects the nature of God, for God is holy. Holy means separate from ordinary daily life and free from the limited, sometimes negative and always ambiguous qualities we associate with life. As a theological statement "God is holy" means that God is special, pure, good and unlike limited humans. For humans holiness means freedom from sin, that is, from the destructive tendencies and behavior which harm human life and community and which mar our relationships with one another and make life unhappy. Thus, for humans holiness has a moral dimension which is joined to the ritual and theological dimensions described previously.

Paul alludes to all these complex practices, rules and attitudes associated with sacrifice, and to the Passover sacrifice in particular, when he calls on the Corinthians to engage in appropriate ethical behavior because of their relationship to Christ, the waiting Passover sacrifice. Passover, which is a central symbol for life, sets the community boundaries by suggesting the social and moral relationships which must emerge when people believe in Jesus Christ. Just as dissensions and conflicts are unacceptable at the Eucharistic meal (chapter 11), so immoral behavior conflicts with the purity of new unleavened bread and the ever present, saving Passover sacrifice, Christ.

## The First Letter of Peter

References and allusions to Exodus are common in the New Testament along with allusions to the Passover. Nowhere else is Passover as explicitly referred to as it is in Paul's First Letter to the Corinthians and in the Gospels. However, Passover is so common and taken for granted in early Christianity that it serves as a stock symbol for various aspects of Christian life. One of the clearest allusions to Passover comes in the First Letter of Peter 1:19. 1 Peter was not written by Jesus' disciple Peter, but much later in the first century by an unknown author who drew upon Peter's authority and reputation to encourage a group of Christian communities in Asia Minor (modern Turkey) to live holy and good lives. Though 1 Peter is cast in a letter form, as are most of the other documents in the New Testament outside the Gospels, its contents are really an exhortation or a homily. The frequent references and allusions to baptism have led some to surmise that the contents of 1 Peter were originally developed as an instruction for those about to be baptized.

After reminding his audience of the salvation and hope they have received in Jesus, the author of 1 Peter urges them to live holy lives: "Do not be conformed to the passions of your former ignorance, but as he who called you is holy, be holy yourselves in all your conduct; since it is written, 'You shall be holy, for I am holy' " (1 Pet 1:14–16). Just as God's holiness required a holy place, the Temple, and ritual purity, it also required holy conduct of Israel and now of the Christian communities. The transition from a previous way of life to faith in Jesus and the Christian way of life involves a separation from previous norms, attitudes and behavior.

The reason for the change of life and separation from what is contrary to God becomes clear through an allusion to Christ as Passover lamb.

> You know that you were ransomed from the futile ways inherited
> from your fathers, not with perishable things such as silver or gold,
> but with the precious blood of Christ, like that of a lamb without
> blemish or spot (1:18–19).

Ransom as a figure for redemption is used by Paul in Romans (3:24) and also in a chapter of Isaiah which dates from the Jewish exile in Babylon (52:3). The members of the Christian community have been bought back from evil by God, and not with the ordinary medium of exchange, gold and silver, but with a sacrifice. The blood of Christ, offered in sacrifice, is compared to the blood of lambs offered in the Temple. The preeminent lamb which saved Israel is of course the Passover lamb in Egypt and in all celebrations subsequently. Both the Passover lamb (Ex 12:5) and any lamb offered at the Temple (Lev 22:19–25) had to be perfect, without any ritual blemishes. Christ is this perfect offering. What does Christ's death bring? "Through him (Christ) you have confidence in God, who raised him from the dead and gave him glory, so that your faith and hope are in God" (1:21).

The religious language concerning Temple, holiness, ransom, faith and a new way of life must not be construed within the narrow confines of individual conscience or weekly worship. 1 Peter frequently refers to the Christian community as God's household and to the Christians as exiles and aliens from ordinary society. Most probably this reflects the new Christians' experience of life in society. They really had to break off social relationships and live a different kind of life to be Christians. Not just their private code and attitudes changed, but their public behavior also, causing painful tensions and worrisome danger. Thus the hope which comes from God and the status they have because of the sacrifice of Jesus must be affirmed and lived in a concrete and difficult way. The Passover sacrifice and salvation symbolized their lives.

## The Letter to the Hebrews

The Letter to the Hebrews is not really a letter, but a complex and beautiful essay on Jesus as Savior and on the kind of Christian life which should follow from faith in Jesus. Hebrews sees Jesus as the final high priest, offering sacrifice for sin in the heavenly, perfect temple. All earthly sacrifice and the Jerusalem Temple itself have been replaced by Jesus' perfect sacrifice for sin. The primary analogue for Jesus' sacrifice in Hebrews is not the Passover sacrifice, but the yearly sacrifice offered for sin by the high priest on the Day of Atonement. On this festival day alone the high priest entered the inner chamber of the Temple, the holy of holies, and offered incense to God for the sins of Israel. Also the famous scapegoat was symbolically burdened with the sins of Israel and driven into the wilderness while a companion goat was offered on the altar.

Just as the author of Hebrews sees the Temple and its sacrifices as leading to Jesus and his unique sacrifice, so he sees the history of Israel and the faith of all its leaders as leading to Christian faith. In the review of Israel's history and faith (in chapter eleven) we find references to the Exodus and Passover. At the beginning of the chapter, faith, which has a wide and rich range of meaning, is defined in this context: "Faith is the assurance of things hoped for, the conviction of things not seen. For by it the men of old received divine approval" (11:1–2). The author then begins his litany with creation itself which is understood by faith. The orientation and goal of the author become clear at the end where he sums up the list: "And all these, though well attested by their faith, did not receive what was promised, since God had foreseen something better for us, that apart from us they should not be made perfect" (11:39–40). The "us" is, of course, Christians who believe in Jesus. The whole Old Testament leads to Jesus and the salvation he brings to Christians, according to Hebrews.

The author reviews numerous figures from the Bible, including Moses. Moses' life manifested faith in four events. Those who hid Moses to protect him from death acted by faith. Moses acted by faith when he refused to accept status as the son of Pharaoh's daughter, but joined his people in their ill-treatment. In this his faith was oriented toward Christ, for "he considered the abuse suffered for the Christ greater wealth than the treasures of Egypt, for he looked to the reward" (11:26). By faith he left Egypt after protecting an Israelite, even though he incurred the anger of the Pharaoh. And finally, "by faith he kept the Passover and sprinkled the blood, so that the Destroyer of the first-born might not touch them (the Hebrews)" (11:28). Note that the Passover lamb and its blood which protects the Hebrews, is not linked to the blood of Jesus, the way it is in 1 Peter. However, all God's actions which protect Israel and which were received in faith by the ancient Israelites looked forward to and led to Jesus' actions which save the Christian community and all humanity. According to Hebrews the whole of the Old Testament, Passover included, is incomplete and a preparation for Jesus and his sacrifice which finally and completely save us from all that is evil.

## The Binding of Isaac

The striking and troubling story of the binding of Isaac, or sacrifice of Isaac, is told in Genesis 22. To test Abraham God commands him to take

Isaac, his only son by Sarah, to a mountain, sacrifice him on an altar and burn the body as a whole offering. (The *binding* of Isaac refers to his being bound on the altar of sacrifice by Abraham in Genesis 22:9.) Abraham proceeds to carry out God's command without understanding it. God's command was especially troubling because Isaac was to be Abraham's descendant who inherited the promises of a land and a great nation which God had made previously. God stops Abraham from sacrificing Isaac at the last minute and reaffirms his promise to Abraham because of Abraham's obedience. The shocking nature of God's test and the repulsive act which Abraham almost commits have fostered numerous Jewish and Christian interpretations and explanations. In Jewish literature the binding of Isaac has been associated with Passover. In the New Testament the binding is related to Jesus and his faithful followers. Though the story is not specifically about Passover, its themes are similar to Passover themes and the two stories have interacted in the tradition.

We will first look at some Jewish traditions concerning the binding of Isaac so that we can better understand the Christian references to this story in the New Testament. The Book of Jubilees, from the second or third century B.C., dates the binding of Isaac to the fifteenth of Nisan, that is, the day of Passover. It identifies Mount Moriah (a geographically unknown place) with Mount Sion, the hill in Jerusalem where the Temple was later built. Finally, it says that Abraham celebrated a seven day festival yearly to commemorate the event. The seven days beginning with the fifteenth of Nisan are the feast of Unleavened Bread.

The Targums are translations of the Hebrew text of the Old Testament into Aramaic, the common language of the Palestinian Jews in the first few centuries A.D. We have several versions of these translations. Even though all the Targums we have are later than the time of Jesus, they probably contain earlier traditions, some of which were current in the first century. The Targums often paraphrased the biblical text and added to it. If something was unclear, they clarified it; if something was "left out," they completed the story. In addition, they often added interpretative traditions to the biblical stories and melded them into one whole.

According to one targumic passage four nights are crucial for the salvation of the world by God: the night of creation, the night of the binding of

Isaac, the night of Passover and the night of the end of the world. Creation and the end of the world stem from God's direct action on all humans. Passover is the moment when God saved the Hebrews and led them out of Egypt to become a nation. But the binding of Isaac is no such national or cosmic event. What special significance does the author see in it? Another targumic passage gives us an insight into the importance of the binding when it says that God listens to Israel's cries for help and salvation because of the merit which Abraham earned when he was willing to sacrifice his only son to God. A later Jewish commentary on the Book of Exodus called the Mekilta makes the saving power of the binding more explicit. In Exodus 12:13 the phrase "When I see the blood" refers to the blood of the Passover lamb smeared on the doorposts of the Hebrews. When God sees this blood, he does not kill the first-born children. However, the Mekilta interprets this phrase to mean, "When I see the blood of Isaac." The binding of Isaac and the "blood" of Isaac are what really move God to spare the Hebrews, not the blood of a mere lamb. In this rabbinic interpretation Israel was really saved at Passover by Abraham's faith and obedience.

This stress on the value of Abraham's action in being willing to sacrifice Isaac creates an interesting enigma. Abraham did not sacrifice Isaac, according to the biblical text. Rather, he found a ram caught in some bushes and sacrificed him. However, the previous interpretation refers to the *blood* of Isaac. Later interpretations speak of the ashes of Isaac and some understand that Isaac was actually sacrificed because in Genesis 22:19 Isaac is not listed among those who returned home with Abraham. Abraham's willingness to sacrifice his son is such an extreme case that it has tremendous power and allows later commentators to speak of it as an actual sacrifice. No wonder the binding of Isaac with its Passover associations finds its way into the New Testament. God was willing to sacrifice his son; the son, Jesus, was a willing victim just as Isaac was, according to some Jewish traditions.

## The New Testament

The review of Israel's history and faith in the Letter to the Hebrews (which we examined above for its reference to Passover and Moses) devotes a long section to the praise of Abraham, including his binding of Isaac.

> By faith Abraham, when he was tested, offered up Isaac, and he
> who had received the promises was ready to offer up his only son
> of whom it was said, "Through Isaac shall your descendants be
> named." He considered that God was able to raise men even from
> the dead; hence, figuratively speaking, he did receive him back
> (11:17–19).

The author of Hebrews, like the rabbis, says that Abraham *offered up* Isaac.
His willingness and intention are his most important and admirable act.
Many of the phrases used to describe Abraham and Isaac describe Jesus: the
only son, offered to God, raised from the dead in the context of faith and
promises. Clearly the author of Hebrews has in mind Jesus' own sacrifice at
Passover.

Jesus' saving activity is related to the binding of Isaac in the Letter of
James, which is an exhortation to Christian good works based on faith. Like
Abraham we must believe and then act. Through faith and works we will be
saved, but faith apart from works is barren and false.

> Was not Abraham our father justified by works, when he offered
> his son Isaac upon the altar? You see that faith was active along
> with his works, and faith was completed by his works, and the
> Scripture was fulfilled which says, "Abraham believed God and it
> was reckoned to him as righteousness"; and he was called the
> friend of God.

From the example of Abraham we understand that humans are justified by
works and not by faith alone. Clearly Abraham's righteousness comes from
the God who justifies him, for God revealed himself to Abraham in the first
place, promised him a land and descendants and gave him a son in old age.
In much the same way Jesus obeyed the Father and gave his life to save us.
We are called to respond in faith and deed the way both Abraham and Jesus
did.

Finally, when Paul is expressing his confidence in God's love and saving grace, he alludes to the binding of Isaac through his choice of words.

What then shall we say to this (that we have been justified)? If God is for us, who is against us? *He who did not spare his own Son* but gave him up for us all, will he not also give us all things with him? Who shall bring any charge against God's elect? It is God who justifies; who is to condemn? (Rom 8:31–34).

The phrase "He who did not spare his own son" corresponds almost exactly to the Greek translation of Genesis 22:16 used by Paul: "Because you did not spare your beloved son, I will indeed bless you." In Genesis God praises and rewards Abraham for his obedience. Most probably Paul is thinking of the example of Abraham and Isaac as a parallel to God and his Son.

None of the New Testament references to the binding of Isaac explicitly mentions the Passover. However, the themes of the binding of Isaac correspond to those of Passover, and Jewish tradition has connected the two events with one another. Voluntary sacrifice, salvation by blood, enduring faith in God, salvation from danger, and promises for the future form the core of the binding of Isaac, Passover and the work of Jesus.

### The Book of Revelation

The Book of Revelation is a series of visions revealed to a believer named John who was living on the Island of Patmos off the coast of Asia Minor (Turkey). What John sees in heaven are a series of symbolic figures, things and events. Various catastrophes are predicted for the earth, including the suffering of the just until their salvation by God and the ultimate destruction of all evil. Evil is represented by a dragon who is ultimately defeated in battle by a heavenly figure on a white horse. Throughout the book the angels and the saved in heaven praise God and Christ who will ultimately be victorious.

The most frequent symbolic figure for Jesus Christ in the Book of Revelation is the Lamb who was slain.

Between the throne and the four living creatures and among the elders, I saw a Lamb standing, as though it had been slain, with seven horns and with seven eyes, which are the seven spirits of God sent out into all the earth (Rev 5:6).

The Lamb is clearly a symbolic figure, for if we try to picture it with seven eyes, seven horns and the wounds on its neck from slaughter, we produce a grotesque physical form. The lamb is like one who had been slain. The seven horns are a sign of strength and the seven eyes a sign of the wisdom associated with God's spirit. The image of the Lamb who was slain derives from the animals sacrificed at the Temple and from the special sacrifice which saved Israel, the Passover sacrifice. The word "slain" in Greek refers both to sacrificial slaughter and to murder; in its double meaning it covers both the Passover lamb and Jesus.

The Lamb who was slain is praised in Revelation 5 as one who is worthy to receive "power and wealth and wisdom and might and honor and glory and blessing" (5:12). He is also called the lion of the tribe of Judah and the root of David who has conquered (5:5). Because he has attained such a powerful position by his death, the Lamb can open the sealed scroll which reveals the secrets concerning the end of the world. His association with Judah and David links him with the anointed royal house and suggests that he is the Messiah. His exalted position in heaven likewise identifies him with the Messianic role as ruler of God's Kingdom.

The Lamb who was slain, like Jesus and the Passover lamb, saves. The saved in heaven are described as those "who have come out of the great tribulation; they have washed their robes and made them white in the blood of the Lamb" (7:14). Even though they have been persecuted, the Lamb has saved and purified them by his own death and blood and he cares for them in heaven (7:17). Like the Lamb, the saved conquer their accusers (12:11). The Lamb has ransomed humans by his blood (5:9), a role which calls to mind the Passover lamb and the Suffering Servant who is led like a lamb to the slaughter (Is 53:7). All of these figures are frequently associated with Jesus in early Christian literature. Here in the Book of Revelation the Lamb assimilates all these titles and symbols into an eschatological context. The Lamb who was slain brings about the final salvation of all believers and resolves the problem of evil by destroying its very source.

The image of a lamb brings to mind a passive creature in the power of others. Jesus, when he was crucified and died, did allow himself to fall into the power of evil humans, but now he has conquered. So the Lamb has been inverted into a symbol of power. The Lamb conquers the worldly kings who make war on him (17:14). He is the judge who keeps the book of life (6:16; 13:8). The evil are judged by him and face his wrath (14:10). Just as the weakness of the Hebrews at Passover led to their ultimate success as a nation, so the Lamb's sacrifice and death have led to his exalted position with God in heaven. The Lamb stands near God's throne or sits on a throne next to him. Most of the hymns sung by heavenly creatures are sung to both God and the Lamb. In the end the New Jerusalem, where the saved live, is the bride of the Lamb and they sit down to a wedding banquet, a traditional image for final salvation which is often associated with the Passover meal.

The Book of Revelation envisions the Lamb who was slain as the victorious leader and spouse of the community of believers. In an analogous way Paul expects his community to measure up to the sanctity and symbolism of the Passover lamb which has been slaughtered and awaits them at the banquet table. All of the writings of the New Testament struggle to adequately portray Jesus and to match the community's behavior and attitudes to those demanded by what Jesus has done. Jesus' death, so like the sacrifice of the Passover lamb, saves, and the authors of the New Testament celebrate this in hymn and allusion to the Old Testament while urging their communities to live up to the way of salvation offered through the blood of Jesus.

# 7

# *Passover and Easter*

Easter is the most important feast of the Christian liturgical year. In the Roman Catholic tradition it is anticipated by several weeks of Lent, and the celebration is extended through the Easter season until Ascension and Pentecost. The week before Easter reminds us in detail of the last few days of Jesus' life, culminating in his death on Good Friday. Surprisingly, most of these holy days were not celebrated in the first century and the early second century. Good Friday celebrations began in the fourth century. The baptism of new converts at the Saturday night vigil began in the third century. An independent Easter celebration began in the second century. Here we shall try to understand the early development of Easter and its relationship to Passover.

The origin of Easter is most difficult to trace, and the first century Christian celebrations of Passover and Jesus' resurrection are most obscure. We would expect the earliest Jewish followers of Jesus to continue observing the Jewish Passover and to associate with it some acknowledgement of his death and resurrection. In their weekly worship they observed the Jewish Sabbath and followed the Sabbath at dawn on Sunday with a communal meal celebrating Jesus' resurrection. From this early observance emerged Christian Sunday worship as we know it. Later non-Jewish Christians omitted observance of the Jewish Sabbath and continued the celebration of Sunday as the memorial of the Lord's resurrection. Probably Passover was adapted analogously to Christian needs and beliefs.

To illustrate the difficulty of knowing how first century Christians worshiped we need only remember that we do not know who presided at the

94

Eucharist in the first century. We know from Acts of the Apostles and Paul's letters that early Christians met together for the breaking of the bread. But these authors assume that we, the believing readers, know what happens at the Christian sacred meal, so they never bother to describe it. We do not know how they prayed or sang, except that they commemorated the death and resurrection of Jesus through bread and wine. We are not told the precise structure of community leadership, nor who led the communal prayers. Church structure was not yet developed and set; single bishops did not emerge as community leaders for each city until near the end of the first century and priests much later. The earliest Christians in Jerusalem still worshiped at the Temple and recognized the hereditary Jewish priesthood as leaders in public worship.

A clear and probable description of how the celebration of Easter emerged during the first and second centuries will be sketched, though the evidence is scarce and many particulars remain hypothetical. Customs, themes and motives common to Easter and Passover will be stressed along with the gradual separation of the two celebrations one from the other as the Christian community separated from Judaism. The major questions to be answered concern what the early Christians did to celebrate Passover and Jesus' resurrection, what the celebrations meant to them and how distinctively Christian celebrations finally dominated the community.

## The Development of Easter

The earliest Christian documents both in the New Testament and from the Apostolic Fathers of the Church were written in Greek. They call the death and resurrection of Jesus and the celebration of it "Pascha." This is the Greek equivalent of the Hebrew word "Pesah," which means Passover. We will refer to these early Christian celebrations as the Christian Passover. The earliest followers of Jesus who lived in Jerusalem until the destruction of the Temple in 70 A.D. celebrated the Passover sacrifice and subsequent evening meal in the ordinary way. Though we have no direct evidence, it is likely that they added some remembrance of Jesus' death and resurrection and recalled his last meal with them at Passover time. Whether such practices and prayers were integrated into the Passover meal, added at the end or celebrated the next morning we do not know.

Twenty years after Jesus' death many Gentiles had entered the Christian community. These non-Jews did not keep the Jewish law or observe Jewish feasts. They did not attend synagogue and they would not have been invited to Passover meals with Jews. They were aware of Passover and its significance, as the Gospel traditions show. Some suggest that Paul's communities had a Christian Passover celebration analogous to the Jewish Passover. 1 Corinthians 5:6–8, which we saw in the previous chapter, refers to celebrating Passover with Christ as the Passover lamb. Some even speculate that both Jews, after the Temple was destroyed in 70 A.D., and Gentile Christians ate a Passover meal with roast lamb which had not been sacrificed at the Temple. Christians would most probably have combined this practice with celebration of the Lord's supper. The evidence for this practice is slim and uncertain but discussion of it illustrates the range of possibilities open to the early Christian community.

That Christian patterns of worship borrowed heavily from Jewish models receives indirect proof from what we know of Christian sects called Jewish Christians. Two of these groups, the Ebionites and the Nazaraioi, first come to our attention in the second century when they are treated as heretical by Church leaders. The Jewish Christians preserved a very Jewish way of life while continuing in their belief that Jesus is the Messiah. They held that observance of the Mosaic law was necessary for salvation and so they rejected Paul's teachings. They read the Gospel of Matthew and had their own interpretation of the prophets. They practiced circumcision, observed the Sabbath, faced Jerusalem when they prayed, celebrated the Eucharist with unleavened bread and water and held that Christ came to abrogate worship in the Temple. They understood Jesus to be the Messiah and the prophet of truth, but not God. Consequently, they rejected the virgin birth of Christ (which implies his divinity), but they accepted baptism and remission of sins, as well as purificatory baths. These groups of Jewish Christians continued to exist into the fourth century, especially in Syria, the home of early Christianity. Gradually, they died out because they were cut off from the main body of Gentile Christians who developed the Christian way of life and theology which has led to present forms of Christianity.

## Quartodecimans

The little we know of Jewish Christians gives us a context for understanding early Christian celebrations of Jesus' death and resurrection. In Syria and Asia Minor during the second century (and probably previously during the first) many Jewish and Gentile Christians celebrated the Christian Passover at the same time as the Jewish Passover, beginning on sundown of the fourteenth of Nisan which is the beginning of the fifteenth of Nisan. For this reason they are called Quartodecimans, the Latin for "Fourteeners." They did not eat the Jewish Passover meal but rather fasted in memory of Jesus' death and perhaps in reparation for the rejection of Jesus by the Jews. They also read the story of the first Passover in Exodus 12 and probably engaged in prayers and hymns. At dawn on the fifteenth of Nisan they broke their fast with the Lord's supper which commemorated Jesus' resurrection. This is the earliest account we have for Christian celebration of Jesus' resurrection.

Most probably other Christians throughout the Mediterranean area celebrated Jesus' resurrection with other customs. Some observed the feast on the Sunday evening following the Jewish Passover. This custom adapted the Jewish Passover to the Christian emphasis on Sunday. At the end of the second century Pope Victor I, the bishop of Rome, threatened to impose a single custom on the whole Church, that of celebrating the resurrection of the Lord on Sunday. Consequently, he worked toward suppressing the Quartodeciman practice of celebrating Jesus' passion and resurrection during the Jewish Passover. We can see in Victor's effort the distance which had opened between the earliest, Jewish Christian customs and the later Gentile customs.

Irenaeus of Lyons, a prominent early Christian writer, defended the Quartodeciman practice of keeping a Christian Passover, even though he followed the more Western custom of Sunday observance. Both he and others defended the antiquity and legitimacy of the Fourteeners' customs and successfully urged Victor not to provoke schism because of a difference in observance. Still, the Sunday observance gradually dominated the whole Church and the observance of the fourteenth of Nisan died out in the next two or three centuries.

## Easter

Even though the Sunday observance of Easter dominated the Church from the late second century, its origins are unclear. An exchange between Polycarp and Anicetus in 155 concerning the varied observances of the resurrection makes it certain that Easter was observed by the middle of the century. At the end of the second century Irenaeus testified that Easter, the observance of the resurrection on Sunday, was known in Rome during the bishopric of Sixtus I, about 115–120 A.D. Though we are not sure how Irenaeus knew this, it seems probable that Easter was observed in Rome and elsewhere in the early first century. Whether it was observed in the late first century and where this observance originated, in Rome or elsewhere, is completely unknown. By the third and fourth centuries the celebration of Easter on Sunday preceded by a vigil Saturday night dominated the Church in both the East and West. Only a few Quartodecimans who celebrated the Lord's resurrection on the Jewish Passover remained.

Both the Jewish and Christian Passovers greatly influenced the Sunday Easter celebrations. Most probably those who transferred Easter to Sunday preceded this celebration with a vigil through the night in imitation of the Passover practice of both Jews and early Jewish Christians. To this vigil with its fasting, readings and prayers were added other elements which perdure to the present in the Easter vigil. Salvation from sin was symbolized by the triumph of darkness over light. A deacon lit a lamp with great ceremony during the vigil service as a sign that the evil powers of night and darkness had been conquered by Jesus, the light. The readings of the Christian Passover were continued, especially the account of the first Passover in Exodus 12. To this was added a solemn hymn, the Exultet, celebrating God's salvation of humans from sin through Jesus Christ. After a sermon by the bishop those who had been instructed in Christianity were baptized and confirmed at this one special time of the year. The remembrance of the historical moment of salvation became the personal moment of salvation through baptism for new believers.

In the third century the celebration of Jesus' resurrection was extended for several weeks after Easter until the celebration of Pentecost. This Jewish feast which followed Passover was adapted into a celebration of the resurrection, just as Passover had been. (The third Jewish pilgrimage feast, Tabernacles, which occurs in the fall, never was accepted into the Christian calendar of feasts.) During the fourth century in Jerusalem, as more and more Christians became devoted to the holy places where Jesus had lived the moments before and after his death, the events of Jesus' last week were separated chronologically in the liturgical calendar. The holy week began with Palm Sunday, followed by Good Friday, and finally a Saturday evening vigil with a midnight Mass at the supposed moment of the resurrection. The chronological and historical scheme was extended to the ascension forty days later (according to the chronology in Luke's Gospel). This historical, geographical and chronological emphasis on salvation history was communicated through twelve readings from Scripture beginning with creation. The early, unified celebration of what Jesus had done and accomplished in his suffering, death, resurrection and exaltation was extended and tied closely to past time and place, rather than to present memory and effect.

## The Meaning of Easter

When we wish to determine what the adherents to a religion believe or what one of their feasts means, we usually listen to what they say and watch what they do. But we have no accounts of what Christians said or did during their commemorations of Jesus' resurrection in the first and early second centuries. We must infer what we can from the fundamental symbolism and from shreds of evidence. Before we turn to Passover symbolism a couple of incidents in the Acts of the Apostles will help us to understand some of the activities of the Christian Passover and Easter.

In Acts of the Apostles, chapter 12, Peter is arrested during the Passover festival (the feast of Unleavened Bread). While he is in jail "earnest prayer for him was made to God by the Church" (12:5). An angel miraculously releases Peter from jail during the night, and when he finds himself on the street, he goes to the house of Mary, mother of John Mark, "where many were gathered together and were praying" (12:12). This most probably happened not on Passover evening itself, but during the feast. Nevertheless, the community is praying during the night, in a way similar to the Jewish Passover meal and the later Christian Passover vigil. A vigil involves waiting for something to happen or preparing for something. Most specifically, the community is waiting for God to rescue Peter and to remove the danger from them. But in Acts this concrete danger to Peter is bound up with the Passover celebration in which Judaism as a whole waits for salvation.

In Acts 20, soon after a Passover festival Paul meets with the Christian community at Troas in Asia Minor. On the first day of the week (Sunday) they gathered together to break bread. Because Paul was leaving on the next day, he prolonged his speech until midnight. Then, after Paul miraculously revived someone who had fallen from the window, he went upstairs, broke bread and continued conversing with the people until daybreak (20:7–12). Note that both here and in the previous scene the community is praying and learning during the night, that is, keeping vigil. This theme of "watching and waiting" is found in the Gospels and in other early Jewish and Christian literature also. It is an act of fidelity to God, an admission that the community needs God and a way of readying itself to receive God. At the first Passover and in all subsequent ones Jews kept watch and honored God with prayer and ritual. The early Christian community both at Passover and on its own special day of worship, Sunday, imitated Judaism with evening and night services.

The act of watching and waiting during the night as well as the fast which was kept by those celebrating the Christian Passover has often been associated with waiting for the coming of the Messiah. Though we have no text which proves that the early Christians associated Passover with the coming of the Messiah, some texts, both Jewish and Christian, indicate that this was a common idea. The coming of the Messiah would bring the ultimate salvation of faithful humanity from evil, oppression and injustice. Consequently, expectation of salvation in the future would logically be associated with salvation in the past at Passover. And for Christians Jesus' second coming as Messianic Lord mirrors his resurrection and exaltation as Lord at the end of his lifetime.

Passover is not simply a time of joy and expectation of salvation. It also remembers danger and suffering, both for the Jews in Egypt and for Jesus on the cross. Consequently, early Christians who celebrated the Christian Passover fasted until the Eucharistic meal at dawn. The watching and waiting was filled with mourning for Jesus' suffering and death and with hope for new life through his resurrection. These themes complement each other and probably form the foundation of all later Easter celebrations.

For Christians Jesus replaces the Passover sacrifice offered at the Temple. The evil and oppression to be escaped are no longer Egypt and Pharaoh but sin in all its forms. The events from Israel's history which remain alive and immediate for Jews today were taken from their context by early Christians and adapted to a new story, that of Jesus. Both Jews and Gentiles who believed in Jesus joined in experiencing the new freedom from sin won through Jesus' suffering and death.

## Melito's Passover Homily

Though we have no prayers or descriptions of first and early second century Christian rituals, we do have a mid-second century homily by Melito the bishop of Sardis. This beautiful, almost poetic sermon explains the meaning of the Christian Passover in relationship to the Jewish Passover and explains the meaning of Jesus for those who believe in him. A description of its contents and some key passages will give us a sense of what early Christians believed.

Melito's sermon was preceded by a reading of the account of the first Passover in Exodus 12, and the first part of the sermon is an interpretation of that story. Passover must be understood as referring both to Judaism and Christianity, to the salvation from Egypt and the salvation which comes through Christ's death and resurrection.

> Understand, therefore, beloved,
> how it is new and old,
> eternal and temporary,
> perishable and imperishable,
> mortal and immortal,
> this mystery of the Pascha. (2)

> For instead of the lamb there was a Son,
>         and instead of the sheep a Man,
> and in the Man Christ who has comprised all things. (5)

After this very Christian introduction Melito describes with blood-curdling horror the killing of the Egyptian first-born. He lays great stress on the darkness of the night and the terror of the first-born infants as they are grasped by the angel of death. Melito then meditates on the ironies of the situation and on the underlying reference to Christ which he sees in the whole Passover story.

> O strange and inexpressible mystery!
> The slaughter of the sheep was found to be Israel's salvation,
> and the death of the sheep became the people's life,
> and the blood won the angel's respect.
> Tell me, angel, what did you respect?
> The slaughter of the sheep or the life of the Lord?
> The death of the sheep or the model of the Lord?
> The blood of the sheep or the Spirit of the Lord?
> It is clear that your respect was won
> when you saw the mystery of the Lord occurring in the sheep,
> the life of the Lord in the slaughter of the lamb,
> the model of the Lord in the death of the sheep;
> that is why you did not strike Israel,
> but made only Egypt childless (31–33).

Previously we saw that Jewish teachers said the blood of Isaac, not the blood of the lamb, saved Israel in Egypt. Melito provides the equivalent Christian interpretation: *Jesus* is the real cause of Israel's salvation. Melito then speaks at length on how Jesus has replaced Passover and concludes with a series of contrasts which begin as follows:

> Once, the slaying of the sheep was precious,
> but it is worthless now because of the life of the Lord;
> the death of the sheep was precious,
> but it is worthless now because of the salvation of the Lord;
> the blood of the sheep was precious,
> but it is worthless now because of the Spirit of the Lord. (44)

To draw heavily upon the Jewish feast of Passover and at the same time tear it from its original context and give it a completely new meaning appropriate to the beliefs of the Christian community characterizes not only Melito's homily, but much of the New Testament and early Christian literature. The original symbols and patterns of worship and relationship with God are retained, but their orientation and meaning are altered to fit the dominant principle of Christian interpretation, Jesus the Savior.

In the second and longer part of his homily Melito develops the meaning of Passover for Christians. The Greek "Pascha," which is a transliteration of the Hebrew word for Passover, resembles the Greek verb which means "to suffer." So, inevitably Jesus' passion is connected to the Passover. Jesus' suffering is a response to the problem of sin, so Melito begins with creation and the first sin in order to show the human predicament and need for salvation through Jesus' suffering and death. In the mid-second century when Melito wrote, the collection of writings which we call the New Testament was still being formed. Thus, the book which Melito recognized as the Bible was the Old Testament. He therefore shows that the Old Testament points toward Jesus' sufferings and he links every suffering in the Old Testament with Jesus.

> But first the Lord made prior arrangements for his own sufferings
> in patriarchs and in prophets and in the whole people,
> setting his seal to them through both law and prophets.
> For the thing which is to be new and great in its realization
> is arranged for well in advance,
> so that when it comes about it may be believed in,
> having been foreseen well in advance. (57)

> Therefore if you wish to see the mystery of the Lord,
> look at Abel who is similarly murdered,
> at Isaac who is similarly bound,
> at Joseph who is similarly sold,
> at Moses who is similarly exposed,
> at David who is similarly persecuted,
> at the prophets who similarly suffer for the sake of Christ. (59)

> Look also at the sheep which is slain in the land of Egypt,
> which struck Egypt
> and saved Israel by its blood. (60)

Though Christians today are used to linking the New Testament and the Old Testament thematically, to see Christ this explicitly in the Old Testament and to "take over" the Old Testament totally in the service of Christ seems extraordinary and extreme. However, Melito sees all God's activity culminating in and leading to Jesus Christ. Even God's dealings with Judaism are subordinate to and have meaning only in Jesus.

Melito parallels his argument that Jesus replaces the Passover of the Old Testament with a long attack on the Jews for having rejected Jesus. He reproaches Israel for killing Christ, for not recognizing God's Son and for ingratitude. Israel has sinned by this behavior and has been punished and even destroyed, according to Melito. Such a strong attack on Jews shocks twentieth century Christians who have a communal history of anti-semitism and most recently were horrified by the Holocaust under Hitler in which six million Jews were slaughtered. However, Melito was the leader of a new, small and struggling Christian community, and he had a threefold purpose in both his emphasis on Jesus and his attack on Judaism. First, he, like other Christian writers of the first and second centuries, had to explain the embarrassing fact that the majority of Jesus' own people to whom he preached did not follow him. Paul in Romans 9—11 expressed confidence that God had some mysterious purpose hidden to us. But, Melito and many after him imputed sinful behavior to Judaism. Second, Melito's homily exemplifies the heavy borrowing of themes, prayers, feasts and beliefs which formed the foundation of Christianity. In order to legitimize those borrowings and to claim the Bible and Passover for Christianity Melito claimed that Judaism had served its purpose and was now finished. Finally, Christianity's origin as a Jewish sect and its heavy debt to Judaism in all areas forced it to struggle for its identity by rejecting its parent and claiming that it was the only legitimate community faithful to God. Melito's outlook is understandable, but not appropriate to the Christian Church in the twentieth century.

After the long attack on the Jewish rejection of Jesus Melito completes his homily with praise of Jesus who is risen and glorified. Jesus calls all to himself: "Come, then, all you families of men who are compounded with sins, and get forgiveness of sins." This is probably an invitation to baptism. The invitation continues:

> For I am your forgiveness,
> I am the Pascha of salvation,
> I am the lamb slain for you;
> I am your ransom,
> I am your life,
> I am your light,
> I am your salvation,
> I am your resurrection.
> I am your king. (103)

In the next few lines Jesus is pictured as everything from Creator at the beginning to Lord at the end. The Christian Passover ends with Jesus in glory, just as the Jewish Passover Haggada ends with Israel free and in glory.

## Separation from Judaism

Easter grew from Passover, but during the second and third centuries it broke off from its parent as Christianity did from Judaism. The separation of Christianity from Judaism can be understood theologically as a logical consequence of faith in Jesus Christ as Savior. After Jesus becomes the central figure and symbol of his community of believers, that community molds its life and belief to fit its understanding of Jesus' work and words. The Jewish community, with Torah at its center along with the traditional practices of Judaism, evolves in a different direction, and after two or three generations the differences become significant enough for the communities to split irreparably.

Sociologically the separation of Christianity from Judaism results from the influx of Gentiles who believed in Jesus. These non-Jewish believers overwhelmed those who were born Jews, and they gradually changed the character and center of the Christian community. The Gentile converts absorbed enormous amounts of Jewish belief and practice: a weekly day of worship, the Bible, hymns and prayers, public reading of the Bible, moral norms, festivals, etc., but they detached these practices from their Jewish setting and gave them a new home and meaning. All beliefs and practices gained acceptance and meaning from their relationship to Jesus Christ.

During the second century the Christian Passover began to be celebrated on Sunday, rather than the fourteenth of Nisan. The practice of a vigil in the evening was retained from Judaism, but the celebration of the Lord's supper at dawn became the most important part of the Easter celebration. Other practices and feasts were gradually added, such as the baptizing of new Christians during the vigil.

During the fourth century a dispute arose over how to fix the date of Easter. Previously, both the Quartodecimans and those who celebrated Easter on Sunday had fixed the date of Easter by reference to the Jewish date for Passover. Since Judaism follows a lunar calendar, an extra month must be added to the cycle of twelve every few years. This dependence on Jews to keep the calendar began to rankle certain groups of Christians, and alternate ways of calculating the proper date for Easter, still according to a lunar calendar, were developed. The two most influential were created in great centers of learning, Rome and Alexandria. Disputes over the proper date for Easter continued for several centuries. During this time Dionysius Exiguus (sixth century) tried to create a calendar which began with Christ's birth and from his effort the modern Western calendar with its "year of our Lord (*Anno Domini*)" resulted.

Since control of a religious calendar is one of the jealously guarded privileges of any religion, the fact that Christians in the fourth century wanted to break away from the Jewish calendar demonstrates clearly that Christianity had ceased to identify with its parent religion. Some authors who urged adoption of a Christian calendar argued that it was improper for Christianity to follow a religion which they thought was mistaken. As a result of this desire for separate identity Jews and Christians celebrate Passover and Easter near the vernal equinox in the Spring, but the dates of these two feasts can vary by days or weeks.

Despite all the changes in the first few centuries of Christian life and the even greater changes in subsequent centuries, Easter and many of its practices remain rooted in Passover. The New Testament and later Christian writings use Passover symbolism and allusions to Passover to explain the meaning of Jesus' death and resurrection. The goals of both festivals remain similar and their central symbolic importance within each tradition is comparable.

# 8

# *The Easter Vigil*

The celebration of Jesus' resurrection at Easter arose under the influence of the Jewish celebration of Passover. The Passover lamb symbolizes the suffering and risen Jesus who saves us. Other adaptations and borrowings from Passover continue into the present and can be seen clearly in the Roman Catholic Easter vigil held during Saturday evening or at midnight on Easter. The vigil is the longest and most elaborate liturgy of the year. It retains many ancient practices, some dating back to the second and third centuries. A review of the vigil service will serve as a review of Jesus' relation to Passover and a summary of the Christian transformation of the Jewish feast of Passover. Public worship acts out the beliefs of a community and articulates the symbolic modes of understanding God which have been derived from tradition and modified by the believers. The Easter vigil illuminates Christian belief and the origins of Christian tradition to a unique degree.

The very notion of keeping vigil during the night preceding Easter dawn arises from the biblical regulations for Passover. In a summary of the Passover regulations a biblical editor writes:

> At the end of four hundred and thirty years, on that very day, all the hosts of the Lord went out from the land of Egypt. It was a *night of watching* by the Lord to bring them out of the land of Egypt; so this same night is a *night of watching* kept to the Lord by all the people of Israel throughout their generations (Ex 12:41–42).

Israel was finally released from Egypt when during the night God killed all the first-born of the Egyptians so that Pharaoh would finally agree to let them go. Because the night was a time of salvation and because God kept watch during that night, Israel keeps watch, that is, keeps a vigil in honor of God and in memory of that original night of salvation. The Jewish evening Passover meal and the Christian Easter vigil both respond to this command.

The Christian understanding of Easter as a Passover that commemorates Jesus' death and resurrection which save us can be seen in the invitation to the Easter vigil with which the leader of the community welcomes the celebrants.

> Dear friends in Christ,
> on this most holy *night*
> when our Lord Jesus Christ passed from death to life,
> the Church invites her children throughout the world
> to come together in *vigil* and prayer.
> *This is the Passover of the Lord:*
> if we honor the memory of his death and resurrection
> by hearing his word and celebrating his mysteries,
> then we shall be confident
> that we shall share his victory over death
> and live with him for ever in God.

The name of the feast remains the same, Passover, even though the event has been changed from the redemption of Israel in Egypt to the redemption of all through the death and resurrection of Jesus.

The Easter vigil is divided into four parts: the lighting of the Easter candle, the reading of the word, the baptism of new Christians and the Eucharist. The reading of the word and the Eucharist are the main elements of any liturgy. The lighting of the Easter candle uses the symbol of light for resurrection, salvation from sin and Jesus' victory over evil. The baptism of new Christians actualizes this salvation in the lives of new members of the community.

Light is a primal symbol of life, trust, understanding and goodness in contrast to darkness which suggests death, fear, ignorance and evil. When the leader of the community ignites a new fire in the dark church, he invokes this symbolism with a blessing: "Father, we share in the light of your glory through your Son, the light of the world. Make this new fire holy, and inflame us with new hope. Purify our minds by this Easter celebration, and bring us one day to the feast of eternal light." The blessing of the candle continues the prayer: "May the light of Christ, rising in glory, dispel the darkness of our hearts and minds." Jesus' death and resurrection, our sin and salvation and the community's struggle between evil and good are caught up in the images of darkness and light.

After the Easter candle is held up for all to see, each person's own candle is lit. In the church filled with light, the deacon sings a hymn of praise which explains the meaning of Easter and praises Jesus for what he has done.

> Rejoice, heavenly powers!
> Sing, choirs of angels!
> Exult, all creation around God's throne!
> Jesus Christ, our King, is risen!
> Sound the trumpet of salvation!

The scene is shifted to God's throne room in heaven where Jesus reigns because of his victory over death. All salvation, even that of the original Passover, is attributed to Jesus' death and resurrection and once again the Jewish and Christian Passovers are collapsed into one.

> This is our *Passover feast,*
> when *Christ, the true Lamb, is slain,*
> whose blood consecrates the homes of all believers.
> *This is the night* when first you saved our fathers:
> you freed the people of Israel from their slavery
> and led them dry-shod through the sea.
> *This is the night* when the pillar of fire
> destroyed the darkness of sin.
> *This is the night* when Christians everywhere,
> washed clean of sin and freed from all defilement,
> are restored to grace and grow together in holiness.
> *This is the night* when Jesus broke the chains of death
> and rose triumphant from the grave. . . .

Of this night Scripture says:
"The night will be as clear as day;
it will become my light, my joy."
The power of this holy night
dispels all evil, washes guilt away,
restores lost innocence, brings mourners joy;
it casts out hatred, brings us peace,
and humbles earthly pride.

The night of Jesus' resurrection is identified with the night on which the Israelites were led out of Egypt by a pillar of fire. The light from God brings salvation to Christians now as it did to the Israelites in the past. Jesus is both the Passover lamb and the light that has come into the world. The salvation which Jesus brings is formulated as freedom from sin and the guilt of sin as well as a cosmic victory over evil forces which influence humans and their world. The means by which the redemption from sin is accomplished is typologically the same as that used by God in Egypt: a Passover lamb is sacrificed. But Jesus, the new Passover lamb, rises from the dead and brings eschatological hope and salvation to all who believe in him.

Jewish sources, too, identified all the crucial nights of God's activity with Passover: the biblical interpretation of the four nights, cited in Chapter Four, links together the nights of creation, the binding of Isaac, Passover, and the final salvation at the end. Though God's power is spread over history and manifests itself in many ways, the religious imagination perceives it as one and identifies past and present with the future. Each of these events throws light on the other, and the symbolic and theological understandings implicit in each event enrich and deepen one another.

The second part of the Easter vigil, the reading of God's word from Scripture, carries on this synthesis of history and the community experience of God. Instead of just one reading from the Old Testament, the service contains seven, many of them familiar to us already. The first three tell the stories of creation, the binding of Isaac and the Exodus, three of the events linked in the Jewish interpretation of the four nights. The next three, from the prophets, speak of God's love, God's care and God's wisdom. These are the divine attributes which caused God to create and save humanity. The final Old Testament reading, from the prophet Ezekiel, promises that God

will gather his people back from exile and purify them from sin and diso-
bedience. Within the scheme of the vigil readings, this is fulfilled through
Jesus.

The reading from Paul's letters is taken from Romans 6 where Paul
compares baptism to Israel's passing through the sea during their escape
from Egypt. The themes of death to life, redemption by God and baptism
are central to the Easter vigil. God's people who believe in Jesus are saved
from destruction just as Israel was at the sea. The water of baptism purifies
them from sin; they are immersed in the water, so they die to sin and they
rise to a new life in Christ. Finally, the discovery of the empty tomb and the
message that Jesus has risen proclaim the Gospel: Jesus has made God's loving care effective through his death and resurrection.

The third part of the liturgy is the baptism of new believers into Christ
and the Christian community. The custom of baptizing new members of the
community during the Easter vigil dates from the third century and is a fitting expression of the saving power of Jesus' death and resurrection. On the
night when the community celebrates most directly and most elaborately the
resurrection of Jesus, it also actualizes that power for the people whom Jesus
came to save by baptizing them into Christ.

Baptism marshals another great symbol, water, to give expression to
faith in Jesus and God's saving power. The blessing of the baptismal water
inevitably refers to creation and the Exodus:

> At the very dawn of creation
> your Spirit breathed on the waters,
> making them the wellspring of all holiness. . . .

> Through the waters of the Red Sea
> you led Israel out of slavery,
> to be an image of God's holy people,
> set free from sin by baptism. . . .

> Your Son willed that water and blood
> should flow from his side
> as he hung upon the cross. . . .

May all who are buried with Christ
in the death of baptism
rise also with him to newness of life.

Water cleanses and renews. At the beginning water was creative and in Jesus' death water is saving. As God saved Israel through water at the sea, so Jesus saves all people through the water of baptism.

As a sign of the centrality of baptism all the participants in the liturgy renew their baptismal promises, rejecting Satan and all evil and affirming their allegiance to God. The faith of the community is best summarized by its response to the baptism of new members:

This is the fountain of life,
water made holy by the suffering of Christ,
washing all the world.
You who are washed in this water
have hope of heaven's Kingdom.

Washing with water, Jesus' saving death, and God's Kingdom are all linked in one symbolic whole which expresses what Christ has done, what the community has experienced and how it expresses its faith.

The fourth part of the Easter vigil, the Eucharistic meal, recalls the last supper of Jesus with his disciples and his subsequent death and resurrection. The Eucharist is the ordinary worship of the community, more deeply understood and experienced on this special remembrance of Jesus' Passover. The ritual intensity of this service and this season is expressed by the shout of joy and praise, "Alleluia." This acclamation of God was first used in the Temple in Jerusalem and was brought into Christian worship through the psalms.

The power of the Easter vigil and the centrality of the identification of Jesus with the Passover lamb can be seen in the documents of Vatican II in which the core of Christianity, both Jesus' actions on our behalf and the response we make in faith, are referred to as the paschal mystery. We cannot know God directly; we must understand God by what he does for us. God's saving actions are preeminently known through the Bible and especially

through the central events in the lives of Israel and Christianity: the redemption of Israel from Egypt by God's defeat of Pharaoh on the first Passover
and the redemption of all from sin by Jesus' death and resurrection during
his Passover. The symbols remain constant and the love and action of God
continue. Human participation is ever renewed and the past lives in the
present with hope for the future, for the final Passover meal with the Lamb
when the Kingdom of God will come and all will live in peace and justice
with God.

# Further Reading

## The Jewish Passover Festival

*The Passover Haggadah.* Ed. Nahum N. Glatzer. Schocken Books

> The text of the Passover Seder with an introduction and explanatory notes.

Ruth Gruber Fredman, *The Passover Seder.* Meridian/New American Library

> An anthropological study of Passover symbolism in the light of other religions and cultures.

Joseph Tabory, "The Passover Eve Ceremony: An Historical Outline," *Immanuel* 12 (1981) 32–43.

Abraham Millgram, *Jewish Worship.* The Jewish Publication Society.

Hayyim Schauss, *Guide to Jewish Holy Days: History and Observance.* Schocken Books.

> Millgram and Schauss describe Passover along with all the other Jewish holidays and services.

Lawrence A. Hoffman, "A Symbol of Salvation in the Passover Haggadah," *Worship* 53 (1979) 519–537.

115

## Passover in Christianity

Joachim Jeremias, *The Eucharist Words of Jesus.* Scribner

The major proponent of the thesis that the Last Supper was a Passover meal.

G. Feeley-Harmick, *The Lord's Table: Eucharist and Passover in Early Christianity.* University of Pennsylvania Press.

An anthropological study of the fundamental rituals and symbols.

Stuart G. Hall, *Melito of Sardis: On Pascha.* Clarendon Press.

The text of Melito's famous passover sermon along with an introduction.

Stuart G. Hall, "Melito in the Light of the Passover Haggadah," *Journal of Theological Studies* 22 (1971) 29–46.